MICHELIN
Travel Publications

D0913358

# Washington, DC

WITHDRAWN

must SEES

| | |
|---|---|
| **Chief Editor** | Cynthia Clayton Ochterbeck |
| **Senior Editor** | M. Linda Lee |
| **Writer** | M. Linda Lee |
| **Contributing Writers** | Rebecca Pawlowski, Martha Hunt |
| **Production Coordinator** | Allison M. Simpson |
| **Cartography** | Peter Wrenn |
| **Photo Editor** | Brigitta L. House |
| **Documentation** | Doug Rogers |
| | Martha Hunt |
| **Proofreader** | Margo Browning |
| **Production** | Octavo Design and Production, Inc. |
| | Apopka, Florida |
| **Cover Design** | Paris Venise Design |
| | Paris, 17e |
| **Printing and Binding** | Quebecor World |
| | Laval, Québec |

**Travel Publications**

Michelin North America
One Parkway South
Greenville, SC 29615
USA
800-423-0485
www.michelin-us.com
email: TheGreenGuide@us.michelin.com

**Special Sales:**

For information regarding bulk sales, customized editions and premium sales, please
contact our Customer Service Departments:

**USA** – 800-423-0485          **Canada** – 800-361-8236

**Manufacture française des pneumatiques Michelin**
Société en commandite par actions au capital de 304 000 000 EUR
Place des Carmes-Déchaux — 63 Clermont-Ferrand (France)
R.C.S. Clermont-FD B 855 800 507

**Note to the reader:**

While every effort is made to ensure that all information in this guide is correct and up-
to-date, Michelin Travel Publications (Michelin North America, Inc.) accepts no liability
for any direct, indirect or consequential losses howsoever caused so far as such can be
excluded by law.

Admission prices listed for sights in this guide are for a single adult, unless otherwise
specified.

# Welcome To Washington, DC

Smithsonian Castle on The Mall

# Table of Contents

# Table of Contents

### THE MICHELIN STARS

For more than 75 years, travelers have used the Michelin stars to take the guesswork out of planning a trip. Our star-rating system helps you make the best decision on where to go, what to do, and what to see. A three-star rating means it's one of the "absolutelys"; two stars means it's one of the "should sees"; and one star says it's one of the "sees" —a must if you have the time.

★★★    Absolutely Must See
★★    Really Must See
★    Must See

## Three-Star Sights★★★

The Capitol★★★
Colonial Williamsburg★★★
Franklin Delano Roosevelt Memorial★★★
Great Smoky Mountains National Park★★★
The Jefferson Memorial★★★
Korean War Veterans Memorial★★★
Lincoln Memorial★★★
Longwood Gardens★★★
Monticello★★★
Mount Vernon★★★
National Air and Space Museum★★★
National Gallery of Art★★★
Vietnam Veterans Memorial★★★
The Washington Monument★★★
The White House★★★
Winterthur Museum★★★

## Two-Star Sights★★

Abby Aldrich Rockefeller Folk Art Center★★
Annapolis★★
Arlington National Cemetery★★
Arthur M. Sackler Gallery★★
Baltimore's Inner Harbor★★
Blue Ridge Parkway★★
Brandywine River Museum★★
Brandywine Valley★★
Charlottesville★★
Corcoran Gallery★★
Department of State Diplomatic Reception Rooms★★
DeWitt Wallace Gallery★★
Dumbarton Oaks★★
Freer Gallery★★
Frontier Culture Museum★★
Georgetown★★
Hagley Museum★★
Harpers Ferry National Historic Park★★

## Two-Star Sights★★

Hillwood Museum and Gardens★★
Hirshhorn Museum★★
John F. Kennedy Center★★
Library of Congress★★
Manassas National Battlefield Park★★
National Archives★★
National Aquarium in Baltimore★★
National Museum of African Art★★
National Museum of American History★★
National Museum of Natural History★★
National Portrait Gallery★★
Old Town Alexandria★★
Phillips Collection★★
Shenandoah National Park★★
Skyline Drive★★
Supreme Court★★
United States Holocaust Memorial Museum★★
University of Virginia★★
Washington National Cathedral★★

## One-Star Sights★

Arlington House, The Robert E. Lee Memorial★
Assateague Island National Seashore★
Baltimore Maritime Museum★
Bureau of Engraving and Printing★
City Museum of DC★
Decatur House★
Dupont Circle★
Dwight D. Eisenhower Executive Office Building★
Federal Bureau of Investigation★
Folger Shakespeare Library★
Ford's Theatre and Petersen House★
Frederick Douglass National Historic Site★
Great Falls Park★
Gunston Hall★
International Spy Museum★
Iwo Jima Memorial★
Kreeger Museum★
Luray Caverns★
Maryland's Eastern Shore★
National Arboretum★
National Museum of Women in the Arts★
National Zoological Park★
Nemours Mansion★
The Octagon★
Renwick Gallery★
Rock Creek National Park★
Smithsonian American Art Museum★
Society of the Cincinnati –Anderson House Museum★
St. Michaels★
Textile Museum★
Tudor Place★
Union Station★
Woodlawn Plantation★

Listed below is a selection of Washington, DC's most popular annual events. Please note that dates may change from year to year. For more detailed information, contact Washington, DC Convention and Tourism Corporation (*202-789-7000; www.washington.org*).

## January

| | |
|---|---|
| **Dr. Martin Luther King Birthday Observance** | 202-619-7222 |
| Dept. of Interior | www.nps.gov |

## February

| | |
|---|---|
| **Abraham Lincoln's Birthday** | 202-619-7222 |
| Lincoln Memorial | www.nps.gov |
| **Black History Month** | 202-357-2700 |
| Various locations | |
| **Chinese New Year Celebration** | 202-357-2700 |
| **Washington Boat Show** | 703-823-7960 |
| Washington Convention Center | www.washingtonboastshow.com |

## March

| | |
|---|---|
| **National Cherry Blossom Festival** | 202-547-1500 |
| Tidal Basin | www.nationalcherryblossomfestival.com |
| **St. Patrick's Day Parade** | 202-637-2474 |
| Constitution Avenue | www.dcstpatsparade.com |
| **Washington Home and Garden Show** | 703-823-7960 |
| Washington Convention Center | www.washingtonhomeandgardenshow.com |

## April

| | |
|---|---|
| **Easter Egg Roll** | 202-456-7041 |
| White House Grounds | www.whitehouse.gov |
| **Easter Sunrise Service** | 703-607-8000 |
| Arlington National Cemetery | www.arlingtoncemetery.org |
| **Filmfest DC** | 703-218-6500 |
| Various locations | www.filmfestdc.org |
| **Georgetown House Tour** | 202-338-2287 |
| Georgetown | www.georgetownhousetour.com |
| **Shakespeare's Birthday** | 202-544-4600 |
| Folger Shakespeare Library | www.folger.edu |
| **Thomas Jefferson's Birthday** | 202-619-7222 |
| Jefferson Memorial | www.nps.gov |

## May

| | |
|---|---|
| **Memorial Day Weekend Concert** | 202-619-7222 |
| Capitol (west lawn) | www.nps.gov |
| **Twighlight Tatto Military Parade** | 202-696-3399 |
| The Ellipse | www.army.mil/armyband |

## June

| | |
|---|---|
| **Dance Africa Festival** | 202-269-1600 |
| Dance Place, 3225 8th St. NE | www.danceplace.org |

**Dupont-Kalorama Museum Walk**  202-667-0441
Dupont Circle
**Smithsonian Folklife Festival**  202-357-2700
The Mall  www.folklife.si.edu

## July

**National Independence Day**  202-619-7222
   **Celebration**  www.nps.gov
The Mall

## September

**Ada Day Festival**  202-321-0938
Columbia Rd. & 18th St.  www.adamsmorganday.org
**Annual Open House**  202-537-3129
Washington National Cathedral  www.cathedral.org
**Constitution Day Commemoration**  301-837-3129
Downtown  www.nara.gov
**International Children's Festival**  703-255-1900
Wolf Trap Farm Park, Vienna, VA  www.wolf-trap.org
**Labor Day National Symphony Concert**  202-619-7222
Capitol (west lawn)  www.nps.gov
**Rock Creek Park Day**  202-895-6222
Rock Creek Park  www.nps.gov/rocr
**Spirit of America**  866-239-9425
MCI Center  www.mdw.army.mil

## October

**Columbus Day Observance**  202-619-7222
Columbus Memorial Plaza  www.nps.gov
**Fall Garden & Grounds Tour**  202-456-7041
White House Grounds  www.whitehouse.gov
**Marine Corps Marathon**  703-784-2225
Starts at the Marine Corps
   War Memorial  www.marinemarathon.com
**Washington International Horse Show**  301-987-9400
MCI Center  www.wihs.org

## November

**Veterans Day Ceremonies:**
   Arlington National Cemetery  202-619-7222
   Vietnam Veterans Memorial  202-619-7222
   US Navy Memorial  202-619-7222

## December

**Christmas Celebration**  202-537-5596
Washington National Cathedral  www.cathedral.org
**Lighting of National Christmas Tree**  202-208-1631
   **& Pageant of Peace**  www.nps.gov/whho/pageant
The Ellipse
**White House Candelight Christmas Tour**  202-456-7041
White House  www.whitehouse.gov

# Must Know: Practical Information

## Area Codes

In DC and Maryland, you need to use the area code if you're dialing between two different area codes, but not within the 202 area code. In Virginia, you need to always dial the area code first for any calls.

Washington, DC: 202

Suburban Virginia: 703, 571

Suburban Maryland: 301, 240

Eastern Maryland: 410, 443

## PLANNING YOUR TRIP

Before you go, contact the following tourist organizations in the DC Metropolitan Area for information about sightseeing, accommodations, recreation and annual events.

**Washington, DC Convention and Tourism Corporation**
    1212 New York Ave. NW, Suite 600, Washington, DC 20005
    202-789-7000; www.washington.org

**Washington, DC Visitors Information Center**
    Ronald Reagan International Trade Center Building
    1300 Pennsylvania Ave. NW, Washington, DC 20004
    202-328-4748 or 1-866-324-7386; www.dcvisit.com

**Alexandria Convention and Visitors Association**
    421 King St., Suite 300, Alexandria, VA 22314
    703-838-4200; www.funside.com

**Arlington Visitors Center**
    1234 South Joyce St., Arlington, VA 22222
    800-677-6267; www.stayarlington.com

**Web Sites** – *For a list of helpful Web sites, see back cover flap.*

## TIPS FOR SPECIAL VISITORS

**Disabled Travelers** – Federal law requires that businesses (including hotels and restaurants) provide access for the disabled, devices for the hearing impaired, and designated parking spaces. For information for disabled travelers, contact the Society for Accessible Travel and Hospitality (SATH), 347 Fifth Ave., Suite 610, New York, NY 10016 *(212-447-7284; www.sath.org)*. The Washington, D.C. Access Guide offers specific information for disabled travelers to the DC area *($5; Access Information, Inc., 21618 Slidell Rd., Boyds, MD 20841; 301-528-8664; www.disabilityguide.org)*.

All national parks have facilities for the disabled and offer free or discounted passes. For details, contact the National Park Service *(Office of Public Inquiries, P.O. Box 37127, Room 1013, Washington, DC 20013-7127; 202-208-4747; www.nps.gov)*.

Passengers who will need assistance with train or bus travel should give advance notice to Amtrak *(800-872-7245 or 800-523-6590/TDD; www.amtrak.com)* or Greyhound *(800-752-4841 or 800-345-3109/TDD; www.greyhound.com)*. Reservations for hand-controlled rental cars should be made in advance.

**Senior Citizens** – Many hotels, attractions and restaurants offer discounts to visitors age 62 or older (proof of age may be required). The **American Association of Retired Persons** (AARP) *(601 E St. NW, Washington, DC 20049; 202-424-3410; www.aarp.com)* offers discounts to its members.

## WHEN TO GO

Spring is Washington's peak tourist season, when mild temperatures and the blossoming of the famous cherry trees *(late Mar–early Apr)* attract crowds of visitors. Make hotel reservations well in advance and expect long lines at the major sights during the spring and the hot, humid summer, when long days, extended operating hours for many sights and numerous outdoor events draw tourists. In the fall temperatures are moderate, crowds thin out and the autumn foliage is spectacular. Winter months can bring snow, but severe snowstorms are infrequent in Washington.

### In The News

The city's leading daily paper, the *Washington Post (www.washingtonpost.com)* lists entertainment, special events and attractions for children in the Friday *Weekend* section; the Sunday edition contains a section highlighting the performing arts. the *Post* also publishes the day's congressional and Supreme Court schedules.

### Seasonal Temperatures in Washington, DC (recorded at National Airport)

|  | Jan | Apr | July | Oct |
|---|---|---|---|---|
| Avg. High | 43°F / 6°C | 67°F / 19°C | 88°F / 31°C | 69°F / 21°C |
| Avg. Low | 28°F / -2°C | 46°F / 8°C | 70°F / 20°C | 50°F / 10°C |

### Congressional Visits

Tickets for congressional visits and special tours of some of DC's more popular sights *(listed below)* may be obtained by writing to your senators or representative. As each member of Congress is allotted a limited number of tickets, requests should be made several months in advance. These visits, which are generally scheduled early in the morning, are more extensive than the standard tours and, best of all, you avoid the long lines.

Members of Congress can arrange special tours for the following sites:

Bureau of Engraving and Printing
Capitol Building Gallery
FBI
Kennedy Center
Library of Congress
National Archives
National Cathedral
State Department
Supreme Court
Treasury Department
White House

When writing your Congress member to request tours, be sure to include the following information:

• Name, address & daytime phone number
• Sites you would like to tour
• Number of individuals in your group
• Dates you will be visiting DC

**Visiting Your Senators or Representatives** – If you would like to meet the elected officials who represent you in Congress, you should write two to three months in advance to request an appointment. Call the Capitol *(202-225-6827)* or write:

US Senate
Washington, DC 20510

US House
Washington, DC 20515

# Must Know: Practical Information

## GETTING THERE

**By Air** – The Washington, DC area is served by three airports, two in Virginia and one in Maryland:

**Ronald Reagan Washington National Airport** (DCA) – 4.5mi south of downtown DC, in Alexandria, Virginia *(703-417-8000. www.metwashairports.com)*.

**Dulles International Airport** (IAD) – 26mi west of downtown DC, in Loudoun County, Virginia *(703-572-2700. www.metwashairports.com)*.

**Baltimore-Washington International Airport** (BWI) – Off I-195, 28mi north of downtown DC and 8mi south of Baltimore, MD *(800-435-9294. www.bwiairport.com)*.

**By Train** – Union Station is Washington's only railroad station and offers Amtrak and other rail service. Located near Capitol Hill at Massachusetts and Delaware Aves. NE, the station is accessible by Metrorail (Red Line). Maryland Rail Commuter Service (MARC) operates trains between DC and Baltimore on weekdays. *For schedules and routes, call 800-872-7245 or visit www.amtrak.com.*

**By Bus** – The capital's main bus terminal *(202-289-5154)* is located at 1005 1st St. NE, a short walk from Union Station. *For fares, schedules and routes, call 800-231-2222 or visit www.greyhound.com.*

**By Car** – Washington is situated at the crossroads of several major interstate routes: I-95 (north-south), I-66 (east), Route 50 (west) and I-270 (northwest). These and other roads leading to the capital connect with the Capital Beltway (I-495), which encircles the city at a distance of about 12mi from the center.

| Car Rental Company | Reservations | Internet |
|---|---|---|
| Alamo | 800-327-9633 | www.alamo.com |
| Avis | 800-331-1212 | www.avis.com |
| Budget | 800-527-0700 | www.drivebudget.com |
| Dollar | 800-800-4000 | www.dollar.com |
| Enterprise | 800-325-8007 | www.enterprise.com |
| Hertz | 800-654-3131 | www.hertz.com |
| National | 800-227-7368 | www.nationalcar.com |
| Thrifty | 800-331-4200 | www.thrifty.com |

## GETTING AROUND

**The Quadrant System** – Based on L'Enfant's design, the layout of DC's streets is logical. The focal point of Washington's street system is the US Capitol building. From this prominent landmark, the two cardinal axes—North Capitol and South Capitol streets, and East Capitol Street and the Mall—divide the city into four quadrants: Northwest, Northeast, Southeast and Southwest.

Numbered streets running north-south are laid out in ascending order on either side of North and South Capitol Streets, while lettered streets running east-west begin on either side of the Mall/East Capitol axis. This arrangement gives rise to two sets of numbered streets and two sets of lettered streets. Since the same address may be found in each of the four quadrants, it is imperative that the appropriate designation (NE, SE, SW, NW) be attached to the address to avoid confusion. Avenues bearing the names of the states of the Union run diagonally across the grid pattern and generally radiate from circles named after prominent Americans such as Washington, Sheridan and Dupont.

• *Note the following particularities:* In the NW and SW quadrants there is no A Street owing to the location of the Mall; B Street is replaced by Constitution Avenue (NE and NW) and Independence Avenue (SE and SW); there is no J Street. Lettered streets end at W, beyond which a new alphabetical series begins with two-syllable names (Adams, Bryant, etc.).
*For information about how to find an address in DC, see back cover flap.*

**By Car** – The use of seat belts is mandatory for driver and passengers. Child safety seats are required for children under four years or weighing less than 40 pounds (seats are available from rental-car agencies). Drivers must always yield the right of way to pedestrians. In the city, street parking is limited and parking regulations are strictly enforced. Arterial streets in the District have posted rush-hour restrictions that prohibit parking from 7am–9:30am and 4pm–6:30pm. Parking signs are color-coded: green and white signs indicate hours when parking is allowed; red and white signs indicate hours when parking is not allowed. Parking spaces reserved for specific use by permit only (diplomatic or government vehicles) are reserved 24hrs daily unless otherwise specified.

## Public Transportation

The Washington Metropolitan Area Transit Authority operates a public rapid-transit (Metrorail) and bus (Metrobus) system that links Washington, DC and areas of Maryland and northern Virginia.

**Subway** – The Metrorail subway system, known locally as the Metro, carries commuters to and from the suburbs during peak commuting hours and is a convenient, safe and inexpensive way to get around while sightseeing in the city. *For schedules, fares and details about the subway, see inside back cover.*

**City Buses** – Metrobuses operate daily *(hours differ by route, for more information, call 202-637-7000 or visit www.wmata.com)*. Bus stops are indicated by red, white and blue signs. Buses display the route number and final destination above the windshield. Fares are determined by the time of day and length of trip *(base fare is $1.20; exact fare required)*; fares are higher during peak commuting hours. To request a Metro Visitor's Kit, call 202-962-2733.

**Taxis** – Numerous taxi companies operate under the supervision of the DC Taxicab Commission *(202-645-6018; www.dctaxi.dc.gov)*. When the "TAXI" sign on the roof of the cab is lit, the vehicle is available for hire. DC taxis do not have meters; instead, the fare is calculated according to a zone system that approximates concentric circles radiating from the Capitol. The base cost of a taxi ride within one zone is $5. A zone map with charges is displayed in the taxi, along with a list of passenger rights. There is a radio dispatch service charge of $1.50. If riding as a group, one passenger pays full fare; all others pay $1.50 each. During rush hours, there is an additional $1 surcharge.

## FOREIGN VISITORS

Visitors from outside the US can obtain information from the Washington, DC Convention and Tourism Corporation *(202-789-7000; www.washington.org)* or from the US embassy or consulate in their country of residence. For a complete list of American consulates and embassies abroad, visit the US State Department Bureau of Consular Affairs listing on the Internet at: *http://travel.state.gov/links.html*.

**Entry Requirements** – Starting October 1, 2003, travelers entering the United States under the Visa Waiver Program (VWP) must have a machine-readable passport. Any traveler without a machine-readable passport will be required to obtain a visa before entering the US. Citizens of VWP countries are permitted to enter the US for general business or tourist purposes for a maximum of 90 days without needing a visa. Requirements for the Visa Waiver Program can be found at the Department of State's Visa Services Web site *(http://travel.state.gov/vwp.html)*.

All citizens of nonparticipating countries must have a visitor's visa. Upon entry, nonresident foreign visitors must present a valid passport and round-trip transportation ticket. Canadian citizens are not required to present a passport or visa, but they must present a valid picture ID and proof of citizenship. Naturalized Canadian citizens should carry their citizenship papers.

**US Customs** – All articles brought into the US must be declared at the time of entry. Prohibited items: plant material; firearms and ammunition (if not for sporting purposes); meat or poultry products. For information, contact the US Customs Service, 1300 Pennsylvania Ave. NW, Washington, DC 20229 *(202-354-1000; www.customs.gov/travel/travel.htm)*.

**Money and Currency Exchange** – Visitors can exchange currency at banks in central DC, as well as at **Thomas Cook Currency Services** *(1800 K St. NW; 202-872-1233)* or **American Express Travel Service** *(1150 Connecticut Ave. NW; 202-457-1300)*. To report a lost or stolen credit card: American Express *(800-528-4800)*; Diners Club *(800-234-6377)*; MasterCard *(800-307-7309)*; or Visa *(800-336-8472)*.

**Driving in the US** – Visitors bearing valid driver's licenses issued by their country of residence are not required to obtain an International Driver's License. Drivers must carry vehicle registration and/or rental contract, and proof of automobile insurance at all times. Vehicles in the US are driven on the right-hand side of the road.

**Electricity** – Voltage in the US is 120 volts AC, 60 Hz. Foreign-made appliances may need AC adapters and North American flat-blade plugs.

**Taxes and Tipping** – Prices displayed in the US do not include sales tax (5.75% in DC), which is not reimbursable. It's customary to give a small gift of money—a tip—for services rendered, to waiters (15-20% of bill), porters ($1 per bag), chamber maids ($1 per day) and cab drivers (15% of fare).

### Measurement Equivalents

| Degrees Fahrenheit | 95° | 86° | 77° | 68° | 59° | 50° | 41° | 32° | 23° | 14° |
|---|---|---|---|---|---|---|---|---|---|---|
| Degrees Celsius | 35° | 30° | 25° | 20° | 15° | 10° | 5° | 0° | -5° | -10° |

1 inch = 2.54 centimeters    1 foot = 30.48 centimeters
1 mile = 1.609 kilometers    1 pound = 0.454 kilograms
1 quart = 0.946 liters    1 gallon = 3.785 liters

## ACCOMMODATIONS
*For a list of suggested accommodations, see Must Stay.*

**Reservations Services**
Accommodations Express – 800-277-1064; www.accommodationsexpress.com.
Capitol Reservations – 800-847-4832; www.hotelsdc.com.

# Must Know: Practical Information

Washington DC Accommodations – 800-554-2220; www.wdcahotels.com.
Bed & Breakfast Accommodations Ltd. – 413-582-9888; www.bnbaccom.com.
Alexandria & Arlington Bed and Breakfast Network – 703-549-3415 or 888-549-3415;
www.aabbn.com.

**Hostels** – A no-frills, economical option, the Washington International Youth
Hostel *(1009 11th St. NW; 202-737-2333; www.hostels.com)* charges between $29
and $35/night and is open year-round (250 beds).

**Campgrounds** – Capitol KOA Campground *(410-923-2771 or 800-562-0248;
www.koakampgrounds.com)*.

| Important Numbers | |
|---|---|
| Emergency Police/Ambulance/Fire Department (24hrs) | 911 |
| Police (non-emergency) | 311 |
| Hotel Docs (24hrs) | 800-468-3537 |
| Dental Referral (Mon-Fri 8am-4pm) | 202-547-7615 |
| **24-hour Pharmacies:** | |
| CVS, 6 Dupont Circle NW | 202-785-1466 |
| CVS, 1199 Vermont Ave. NW (Thomas Circle) | 202-628-0720 |
| Poison Control Center (24hrs) | 202-625-3333 |
| Time | 202-844-2525 |
| Weather | 202-936-1212 |

## SPORTS
DC is a great place to be a spectator where sports are concerned. The city's
major professional sports teams include:

| Sport/Team | Season | Venue | Phone/Web site |
|---|---|---|---|
| Baseball (AL)<br>Baltimore Orioles | Apr–Sept | Oriole Park at Camden Yards<br>333 W. Camden St.<br>Baltimore, MD | Info: 410-685-9800<br>Tickets: 888-848-2473<br>www.orioles.mlb.com |
| Football (NFL)<br>Washington Redskins | Sept–Dec | FedEx Field<br>Landover, MD | Tickets: 301-276-6050<br>www.redskins.com |
| Hockey (NHL)<br>Washington Capitals | Oct–Apr | MCI Center<br>7th & F Sts. NW | Info: 202-628-3200<br>Tickets: 202-432-7328<br>www.washingtoncaps.com |
| Basketball (NBA)<br>Washington Wizards | Nov–Apr | MCI Center<br>7th & F Sts. NW | Info: 202-628-3200<br>Tickets: 202-432-7328<br>www.washingtonwizards.com |
| Basketball (WNBA)<br>Washington Mystics | May–Aug | MCI Center<br>7th & F Sts. NW | Info: 202-661-5000<br>Tickets: 202-432-7328<br>www.washingtonmystics.com |
| Soccer (MLS)<br>DC United | Apr–Oct | RFK Stadium<br>E. Capitol & 22nd Sts. SE | Info: 703-478-6600<br>Tickets: 202-432-7328<br>www.dcunited.com |
| Soccer (WUSA)<br>Washington Freedom | Apr–Aug | RFK Stadium<br>E. Capitol & 22nd Sts. SE | Info: 202-547-8351<br>Tickets: 202-432-7328<br>www.washingtonfreedom.com |

# Washington, DC

# Power and Politics: Washington, DC

**T**his is where it all happens: the political wheeling and dealing, the power lunches, the late-night trysts on the Capitol grounds. Politics rule the day in the nation's capital, where power is king and administrations rise and fall at the will of the people.

It all started with George Washington in 1790. Elected America's first president after the new nation won its independence from Britain in the Revolutionary War, Washington was charged with finding a suitable place to locate the seat of government. The spot he chose was a tract of land near the prosperous port of Georgetown. Washington knew this area well—his own plantation, Mount Vernon, lay just 16mi south along the Potomac River.

Washington appointed French major Pierre Charles L'Enfant (1754–1825) to design the new capital. L'Enfant, who fought under General Washington in the Revolution, had formal training in architecture and design. The plan conceived by the Frenchman called for a diamond-shaped federal district that measured 10mi long on each side and encompassed portions of Maryland as well as the county of Alexandria on the west bank of the Potomac River.

One of L'Enfant's first decisions was to situate the future "Congress house" on Jenkins Hill, which commanded a striking view of the Potomac River. Along this east-west axis he planned a 400ft-wide "Grand Avenue" (now The Mall) to be lined by foreign ministries and cultural institutions. The avenue would connect on a north-south axis with the "President's house," which in turn would link back to the Capitol via a mile-long commercial corridor (present-day Pennsylvania Avenue). L'Enfant laid out the rest of the city in a grid pattern of streets intersected by broad diagonal avenues at "round points" (DC's infamous traffic circles).

Despite numerous setbacks, including L'Enfant's dismissal in 1792, Washington was well on its way to becoming a city by the mid-19C. In 1871 the District of Columbia incorporated Georgetown, and improved transportation spurred growth in neighboring Virginia and Maryland.

Today the 10-county Washington metropolitan area fans out in densely settled suburbs reaching north toward Baltimore, Maryland; south toward Alexandria, Virginia; east across the broad estuarine expanse of Maryland's Eastern Shore; and west toward the Blue Ridge Mountains. The rumblings that preceded the Civil War began in the mountains west of Washington in Harpers Ferry, West Virginia *(see Excursions)*. Once the war exploded, some of its most noted battles were fought in the countryside within an hour's drive of the capital.

Conceived as a national showplace, Washington, DC reigns as a truly international city, boasting world-class museums and performing arts, spectacular memorials and fine shopping and dining. As the political heart of the nation, DC is remarkably accessible, opening the doors of Congress, the Supreme Court and other federal institutions to hosts of visitors who come to witness democracy in action.

### A Government For The People

The US Constitution divides the government into three separate branches with varying responsibilities.

Charged with carrying out and enforcing laws and regulations, the **Executive Branch** consists of the president and vice president—both elected together for a maximum of two four-year terms. In addition, 14 cabinet departments, whose heads are appointed by the president, and some 80 separate agencies help carry out executive functions and advise the president on matters of state.

The **Legislative Branch** drafts and passes laws. It is made up of two sections, a **House of Representatives** and a smaller **Senate**, collectively known as Congress. The House, where states are represented according to their population, numbers 435 members. The Senate, on the other hand, contains two members from each of the 50 states, no matter the state's size. In addition to lawmaking, Congress has the power to declare war, levy taxes, regulate interstate commerce and impeach other government officials—including presidents and judges.

Smallest of the three branches of government, the **Judicial Branch** interprets the law of the land. It consists of the **US Supreme Court** (the country's highest court), some 94 district courts and 13 appellate courts.

**A** visit to the nation's capital—the seat of the United States government—promises to be a "gee-whiz" experience. You can't help but be moved when you see how much larger the Capitol building, the White House, the Memorials and other grand government buildings seem when you see them in person. DC is a destination like no other—it's the place where the checks and balances established by the US Constitution still protect the freedoms Americans hold so dear.

## The Capitol★★★

*1st St. between Independence & Constitution Aves. NE. 202-225-6827. www.aoc.gov. Open year-round Mon–Sat 9am–4:30pm. Closed Sun, Thanksgiving Day & Dec 25.*

Icon of democracy in progress, the tiered white dome crowned by the statue of *Freedom* is well known to all Americans. The design of the massive Capitol building, which has served as the home of the US Congress since 1800, resulted from a public competition held by President George Washington and Secretary of State Thomas Jefferson. The winner, Dr. William Thornton, was awarded $500 and a city lot. The cornerstone was laid in 1793, and by 1800 Congress was able to leave Philadelphia—the young republic's temporary capital—and take up residence in the new federal city. Following Thornton's resignation in the early 1800s, the Capitol was completed over the next 30-odd years with the help of architects Benjamin Latrobe and Charles Bulfinch. The building was expanded in the mid-19C by Thomas U. Walter; a hundred years later, Congress had outgrown the Capitol again, and the east facade was extended by 32.5ft.

**Great Rotunda** – The ornate Capitol **dome**★★—180ft high and 90ft across—displays an allegorical fresco, The Apotheosis of Washington, by Constantino Brumidi.

**Main Floor** – Semicircular half-domed Statuary Hall appears (unfurnished) as it did in 1857 when it served as the House Chamber.

**Old Senate Chamber** – The Supreme Court held sway here from 1860 to 1935.

**Ground Floor** – The Crypt holds displays on the Capitol's history. Arched ceilings and walls of the intersecting **Brumidi Corridors** are decorated with Brumidi's murals.

### Watching Democracy In Action

Visits to the Capitol are by guided tour only, except when Congress is in session. Visitors must obtain free timed tickets on the day of their visit, beginning at 9am. Tickets are available at the Capitol Guide Service Kiosk *(Independence Ave. & 1st St. SW)*.

The public only has access to the Senate Chambers or the Hall of the House of Representatives when Congress is in session. US citizens can obtain passes to view a House or Senate session through the office of their state senator or representative. Foreign visitors must apply for passes at the South Visitor Receiving Facility *(near Independence Ave. SW; foreign photo ID required)*.

*Call for schedule and agenda: Senate, 202-224-5456; House of Representatives, 202-225-4000.*

## The White House★★★

*1600 Pennsylvania Ave. NW. 202-208-1631. www.whitehouse.gov. Visit by guided tour only. Closed Sun & Mon. Due to security risks, individual tours have been suspended; for updated information, call the visitor information line: 202-456-7041.*

What American hasn't dreamed of living at the White House? Universal symbol of the US presidency, this Georgian beauty has housed America's presidents and their families beginning with John Adams in 1801.

**Tips For Visiting**

Since tours are currently suspended, check with the White House Visitor Center *(15th & E Sts. NW; open daily 7:30am–4pm)* before planning your visit.

A public contest was held in 1792 to find someone to design the "president's palace" (as DC planner Pierre L'Enfant called it), which today is surrounded by 18 acres of green lawns and flower gardens. Even Thomas Jefferson, a self-taught architect, submitted an entry—anonymously. Jefferson lost the competition, and the $500 prize went instead to a young Irish builder, James Hoban. Although the cornerstone was set in 1792, the house was not completed during President Washington's term in office. So John Adams, the nation's second president, became the first to live in the whitewashed stone mansion.

When James Madison lived here as the fourth president of the US, the British set fire to the White House during the War of 1812. Fortunately, a well-timed rain saved the house from burning to the ground. Over the years, the Executive Mansion has been expanded and redecorated, reflecting the tastes of the First Families who have occupied it for more than 200 years.

| | |
|---|---|
| **First Floor** | Contains formal state reception areas. |
| **East Room** | Hosts concerts, dances and official White House ceremonies. |
| **Green Room** | A drawing room with green watered-silk wall coverings and furniture from the 19C workshop of Duncan Phyfe. |
| **Blue Room** | This elliptical room includes seven of the original Bellange gilded armchairs ordered from Paris by James Monroe. |
| **State Dining Room** | The site of official dinners seats 140. |
| **Second & Third Floors** | These floors contain the First Family's living quarters. |
| **West Wing** | *Not open to the public.* Houses the Cabinet Room, staff and reception rooms, and  the President's Oval Office. |

# Department of State Diplomatic Reception Rooms★★

*23rd St. between C & D Sts. NW. 202-647-3241. www.state.gov/www.about_state/ diprooms. Visit by prearranged guided tour only year-round Mon–Fri 9:30am, 10:30am & 2:45pm. Make reservations four weeks in advance. Closed weekends & major holidays. Tour is not recommended for children under 12.*

To look at the main State Department office building, you'd never guess that inside this undistinguished 1960s structure hide masterpieces of 18C interior design. Used for official functions hosted by the secretary of State and other high-level government officials, the Diplomatic Reception Rooms are furnished with one of the country's most impressive collections of 18C **American decorative arts**★★ dating from 1750 to 1825.

When the State Department headquarters building opened in 1961, its eighth-floor reception rooms were furnished in a stark, streamlined decor in keeping with the building's concrete-and-glass modernism. Shortly thereafter, the Americana Project, under the direction of the Fine Arts Committee of the State Department, was begun to upgrade these areas through private donations. Georgia architect Edward Vason Jones dedicated the last 15 years of his life to redesigning the rooms in the style of great 18C American manor houses.

**Best Rooms in the House** *(Diplomatic Reception Rooms are located on the 8th floor)*

**Edward Vason Jones Memorial Hall** — This elegant foyer is appointed with faux marble pilasters and cornices, and gray marble floors.

**Entrance Hall** — Adjoining Memorial Hall, the Entrance Hall contains the oldest dated and signed piece of bombé furniture in North America; it was made by Benjamin Frothingham of Charlestown, Massachusetts in 1753.

**John Quincy Adams State Drawing Room** — The secretary of State greets official guests in this 18C-style drawing room, with its hand-carved architectural details. Here you'll find the English Sheraton desk where John Jay signed the Treaty of Paris in 1783.

**Thomas Jefferson State Reception Room** — Its perfect Neoclassical proportions reflect Jefferson's own architectural tastes.

**Benjamin Franklin State Dining Room** — Largest of the Diplomatic Reception Rooms, the ornate State Dining Room was redesigned by John Blatteau in 1985 with red-veined scagliola marble columns running the length of the room. An 8,000-pound Savonnerie rug covers the floor; on the ceiling, eight cut-glass chandeliers flank the Great Seal of the US, fashioned in plaster and gilt.

## Library of Congress★★

*1st St. & Independence Ave. SE. 202-707-5000. www.loc.gov. Thomas Jefferson Building open year-round Mon–Sat 10am–5:30pm. Call for hours for James Madison and John Adams buildings. All library buildings are closed Sun & major holidays.*

Imagine the largest library in existence and you've got the Library of Congress. Its collection numbers a mind-boggling 120 million items—now that's a lot of reading material! Established in 1800 (and housed in the Capitol) for the exclusive use of Congress, the library became a public institution in 1864 under the direction of Librarian of Congress Ainsworth Rand Spofford. A separate building—now known as the **Thomas Jefferson Building**★★—for the library opened in 1897; it has served as the "national library of the United States" ever since.

### A Library For The People

The Library of Congress is open to the general public and functions as a reference library for individuals 18 years or older. An orientation video is shown regularly in the visitors center *(ground floor, Jefferson Bldg.)*. Free guided tours of the Jefferson Building are available. A cafeteria *(open to the public for lunch)* is located on the 6th floor of the Madison Building.

For visitor information or assistance in using the research facilities, consult the touch-screen terminals in the visitor center.

**Visitor information**: 202-707-8000.

**Research information**: 202-707-6500.

**Tour information**: 202-707-9779.

A richly ornamented Beaux-Arts-style landmark, the Jefferson Building fills an entire square block across from the Capitol. Together with the 1939 Art Deco **John Adams Building** *(2nd St. SE, behind the main building)* and the austere 1980 **James Madison Memorial Building** *(Independence Ave., between 1st & 2nd Sts. SE)*, the three structures that make up the Library of Congress hold more than 18 million books, 27 million manuscripts, 4 million maps and atlases, and 8 million musical items.

**Great Hall** – The Jefferson Building's two-story Great Hall is noted for its gold-leaf ceiling and vaulted corridors. Here you'll find a copy of the mid-15C Giant Bible of Mainz—one of the last hand-illuminated manuscript versions of the Bible.

**Main Reading Room** – An elaborately sculpted grand staircase leads to the second-story colonnade, where a visitors' gallery overlooks the Main Reading Room—a vast rotunda under the library's massive copper dome (160ft from floor to lantern). The room is ringed by Corinthian columns and arched windows embellished with stained-glass state seals and eagles.

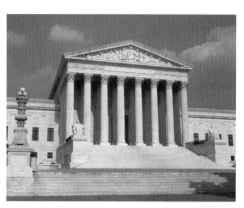

## Supreme Court★★

*1st & E. Capitol Sts. NE.*
*202-479-3211.*
*www.supremecourtus.gov.*
*Open year-round daily 9am–*
*4:30pm. Closed weekends &*
*major holidays.*

Located across the street from the Capitol, the highest court in the land has the last word in many a court case. The Court was established by Article III of the US Constitution, ratified in 1788, which called for a "supreme court" to have the final decision in matters of law and to act as a counterbalance to the legislative and executive branches of government.

In 1790 the first US Supreme Court met at the Royal Exchange Building in the temporary capital of New York City. In 1800 it moved to DC and occupied several different rooms in the Capitol over the years. William Howard Taft, the tenth chief justice (1921–1930) and the only US president to serve on the Court, convinced Congress in 1828 to set aside funds for a building to house the Court. More than a century later (October 1935), the present cross-shaped marble structure, designed by Cass Gilbert, was completed.

Nine justices, who are appointed by the president with Senate approval, serve on the Supreme Court. Only death, voluntary retirement or resignation, or congressional impeachment can remove a sitting justice.

### Justice For All

The Court's term begins on the first Monday in October. From October through April the Court hears oral arguments on cases it has agreed to review. Of the 7,000-some requests for review it receives annually, the Court hears only 75–100 cases. It typically sits two weeks a month *(Mon–Wed)*. From mid-May through June the Court convenes on Monday to deliver its opinions on cases argued during that term.

Court sessions are open to the public on a first-come, first-served basis. Check the *Washington Post* for the daily schedule of hearings.

### Best of the Supreme Court Building

• Two James Fraser sculptures, representing the Contemplation of Justice (*left*) and the Authority of Law (*right*), flank the broad staircase in front of the Supreme Court.

• Within the huge courtroom chamber, justices sit on a raised bench ringed by massive columns. The justices' places are ordered by their seniority, with the chief justice taking the center position.

• A statue of **John Marshall** (1755–1835), the "Great Chief Justice" who held the post from 1801–1835, dominates the main hall on the ground level.

## Bureau of Engraving and Printing ★

*14th & C Sts. SW. 202-874-3019. www.moneyfactory.com. Visit by guided tour only year-round Mon–Fri 9am–2pm & 5pm–7pm. Closed weekends & major holidays.*

### The Color of Money

Green ink was chosen for one side of America's original paper currency because of its resistance to physical and chemical change, earning these early notes the name "greenbacks." In 2003 the Bureau of Engraving and Printing together with the Federal Reserve will introduce redesigned notes. The new notes, which are intended to deter counterfeiters, will use color-shifting ink that changes color when the note is tilted.

If you get a thrill from being surrounded by money, this is the place to be. "The nation's money factory" produces paper currency, postage stamps and many of the official documents issued by the US government. Located at the foot of the 14th Street Bridge, the Bureau of Engraving and Printing turns out 37 million notes a day with a face value of approximately $696 million.

Established in the years after the Civil War, the Bureau of Engraving and Printing was responsible for all currency printing by 1878. In addition to bills and postage stamps, the bureau also produces Executive and Treasury seals, official engravings of presidents and governmental buildings, presidential invitations and military certificates.

### Tour Highlights

The entrance hall contains displays and a 15-minute film on the history of currency and US paper-money production. The remainder of the tour leads past three processing rooms. The tour ends in an exhibit hall displaying stamps, bills and historical materials. Visitors must obtain same-day free tour tickets from the kiosk on the bureau's 15th St. side, beginning at 8am.

- In the **first room**, bills are printed by a process called intaglio printing, whereby impressions are made by pressing inked engravers' plates into the currency fabric—a blend of cotton and linen. Each fabric sheet holds 32 bills.

- In the **second area**, sheets are trimmed and examined for imperfections. Any defective sheets, or "muts" (an abbreviation of mutilated), are shredded.

- The **third room** is devoted to printing Treasury seals and serial numbers on the bills. After this final printing the bills are cut, stacked and banded before they are distributed to the 12 Federal Reserve banks throughout the country.

# Dwight D. Eisenhower Executive Office Building★

*17th & G Sts. NW. 202-395-5895. www.whitehouse.gov/history/eeobtour. Visit by guided tour only. Tours currently suspended until further notice. Closed major holidays.*

Picture a tiered wedding cake rising to the west of the White House. This is the massive Executive Office Building, one of Washington's architectural treasures. After years of neglect, its wall stencilling, cast-iron detailing and English Minton tile floors have all been restored to their former glory. The building now houses several key government offices of the Executive branch, including the Executive Office of the President, the Office of Management and Budget, the National Security Council, and the Office of the Vice President.

Erected as headquarters for the departments of State, War, and Navy, this grand building symbolized the renewed vitality of the government after the Civil War. It was designed in the French Second Empire style by architect Alfred Mullett. Sumptuous offices have provided a splendid workplace for scores of noted government figures over the 20C. Theodore and Franklin D. Roosevelt, William Taft, Herbert Hoover, Dwight Eisenhower, Lyndon Johnson, Gerald Ford and George H. Bush all maintained offices here at some point in their careers before moving into the executive mansion next door.

## Dwight's Delight

When it was built in 1888, the Executive Office Building was Washington's largest and most lavish office building. Its remarkable features include:

- 900 exterior columns
- 1,572 windows
- More than 550 rooms
- Nearly 2 miles of corridors
- 4½ft-thick granite walls

**Executive Office of the President Library** – Four stories of alcoves with cast-iron balconies enclose the central reading area, whose lovely gold and white vaulted ceiling is decorated with original stencilling.

**Indian Treaty Room** – Originally the Navy's library and reception room, the chamber's décor reflects a number of nautical motifs. President Eisenhower held the first televised presidential press conference here in 1955.

**Vice President's Ceremonial Office** – Used by the vice president for meetings and interviews, this ornate room, with its Belgian black-marble fireplaces and stenciled walls formerly served as the office of the secretary of the Navy.

## Federal Bureau of Investigation★

*E St., between 9th & 10th Sts. NW. 202-324-3447. www.fbi.gov.*
*Visit by guided tour only; tours suspended until renovation is complete. Closed weekends and major holidays.*

You've seen it dramatized on TV. You've read about it in the newspapers. Now you can see for yourself why the FBI has long been the stuff of legend in American minds. Since it started holding tours in 1937, the FBI has treated visitors to a peek at the inner workings of the agency that—under the 48-year leadership (1924–1972) of director J. Edgar Hoover—became the supreme federal authority in matters of domestic crime.

The principal investigative arm of the Justice Department, the FBI traces its beginnings to 1908, when a permanent force of special agents was placed under the control of the attorney general. In 1935 this force was designated the Federal Bureau of Investigation and its powers were broadened in an effort to stop the gangsters who were operating networks of organized crime.

Officially known as the J. Edgar Hoover FBI Building, the FBI's fortresslike headquarters building (completed in 1975) covers a city block and houses some 9,800 workers. In addition to this building, the FBI maintains 56 field offices, 400 satellite offices, and more than 40 foreign liaison posts, while employing 11,400 special agents.

### FBI's Top Five Priorities

1. Protect the US from terrorist attack.
2. Protect the US against foreign intelligence operations and espionage.
3. Protect the US against cyber-based attacks and high-technology crimes.
4. Combat public corruption at all levels.
5. Protect civil rights.

### Tour Highlights

*Tours suspended until fall 2004 for renovation. The new tour will bring some of the Bureau's most famous cases to life through multimedia presentations.*

- Core exhibits detail the history and procedures of the FBI. Additional exhibits focus on the Bureau's Ten Most Wanted criminals, white collar crime, illicit drugs and organized crime.

- **FBI Laboratory** anaylzes more than 1,000,000 pieces of evidence each year, including bullets, firearms, paint and fibers.

- **Live firearms demonstration** by an FBI special agent concludes the tour. The Bureau retains a reference collection of 5,000 weapons, most of which were seized from apprehended criminals.

Y ou may groan when you hear the word "museums," but with choices from art to zoology—and everything in between—DC's museum offerings are bound to please even the most hardened culture-phobe. The capitol's cultural heart and the world's densest concentration of museums lie along the east end of the **National Mall**★★★, the mile-long, tree-lined esplanade extending from the foot of Capitol Hill to 15th Street. Here you'll find the many museums of the **Smithsonian Institution** *(no admission fee)*, established in 1846 with an endowment from prominent English scientist James Smithson.

## National Air and Space Museum★★★

*6th St. at Independence Ave. SW. 202-357-2700. www.nasm.si.edu.*
*Open year-round daily 10am–5:30pm. Closed Dec 25.*

Who hasn't dreamed they could fly? From the Wright Brothers' *1903 Flyer* to John Glenn's space capsule *Friendship 7*, the milestones of man's fascination with flight are presented here at the world's most visited museum. Established in 1946 to "memorialize the national development of aviation," the National Air and Space Museum (NASM) contains the world's most comprehensive collection of aircraft, spacecraft and flight-related artifacts. Architect Gyo Obata designed the Tennessee-marble-faced structure that opened for the nation's bicentennial in July 1976.

The 23 galleries contained within the building's four massive rectangles contain hundreds of aircraft and spacecraft, rockets, guided missiles and satellites, as well as exhibits that trace the history of flight from its earliest days through World War II and into the space age. Be sure to try your hand **At the Controls of Flight Simulator Zone**, where you can execute gut-wrenching aerobatics aboard the MaxFlight® RS2000 simulator. Don't leave without a virtual soar through the sky in NASM's classic movie *To Fly* shown on the five-story screen of the Lockheed Martin IMAX® Theater.

**Milestones of Flight** – Occupying the central part of the building, this hall displays such epoch-making aircraft as Charles Lindbergh's Ryan NYP, *Spirit of St. Louis,* and Chuck Yeager's Bell X-1, *Glamorous Glennis.*

**Explore The Universe** – The museum's newest permanent exhibit takes you through four centuries of man's observations of the galaxies, and showcases astronomers' tools from 11C Islamic astrolabes to the Hubble Space Telescope.

## Steven F. Udvar-Hazy Center

Designed to coincide with the anniversary of the Wright Brothers' first manned, powered flight, the National Air and Space Museum opens its newest facility on 175 acres adjacent to Dulles International Airport in December 2003. The Udvar-Hazy Center, named for its major benefactor, displays more than 200 aircraft and 135 spacecraft in its 70,600sq ft building. Inside the aviation building, visitors have access to elevated walkways from which they can view aircraft displayed on the floor and suspended above from two levels. An observation tower provides a great viewpoint for visitors to watch planes land and take off from Dulles Airport.

### Flight Firsts

**Early 16C** – Leonardo da Vinci studies bird flight and draws plans for flying devices.

**1783** – First manned balloon flight by the Montgolfier brothers in Paris.

**1896** – First successful engine-driven craft flight by Samuel Langley's Aerodrome No. 5 in Washington, DC.

**1903** – Wilbur and Orville Wright make the first successful motorized flight at Kitty Hawk, North Carolina in their *1903 Flyer.*

**1909** – Louis Blériot crosses the English Channel in 36 minutes in a Type XI monoplane.

**1911** – G.P. Rodgers makes the first coast-to-coast flight in the Dutch-built Fokker T-2.

**1927** – Charles Lindbergh makes the first solo nonstop crossing of the Atlantic in his Ryan NYP, *Spirit of St. Louis.*

**1932** – Amelia Earhart becomes the first woman to make a solo nonstop transatlantic flight.

**1947** – Air Force pilot Chuck Yeager breaks the sound barrier in his Bell X-1, *Glamorous Glennis.*

# National Gallery of Art★★★

*Madison Dr., between 3rd & 7th Sts. NW. 202-737-4215. www.nga.gov.*
*Open year-round Mon–Sat 10am–5pm, Sun 11am–6pm. Closed Jan 1 & Dec 25.*
*Sections of the National Gallery may be closed for renovation.*

You'll want to make a beeline for this place if art is your passion. Even if it's not, you're bound to find something you like among the more than 3,200 paintings, 2,600 pieces of sculpture, 560 pieces of decorative art and 98,000 works on paper in the National Gallery's collection. A world-class art institution, the National Gallery traces the development of Western art from the Middle Ages to the present. Its holdings have mushroomed from a core of 126 paintings and a group of fine 15C–16C Italian sculptures  stately marble West Building (1941) that graces the Mall; today gallery operations are supported by federal monies.

**West Building** – Renowned architect John Russell Pope designed this domed Classical Revival structure, the exterior of which glows with seven shades of pink Tennessee marble. Arranged in chronological order, galleries on the main floor of the West Building progress from a superb group of 13C–15C Italian Painting through Spanish, German and Flemish masterpieces to 19C French Painting. Works by Thomas Gainsborough and J.M.W. Turner are included among the collection of British Painting, while the portraiture of Benjamin West, Charles Willson Peale and Gilbert Stuart highlight the American Painting galleries.

**East Building**★★ – In the 1970s the Mellon family again came forward to endow the museum's acclaimed East Building (1978, I.M. Pei), which is devoted to late-19C and 20C art. Considered the most impressive example of modern architecture in Washington, the East Building *(entrance on 4th St. across the plaza from the West Building)* opens into a soaring skylit atrium dominated by an immense red, blue and black mobile by Alexander Calder, which was specially commissioned for this space. Five floors of open, fluid gallery space showcase the work of Pablo Picasso, Wassily Kandinsky, Mark Rothko and Georgia O'Keeffe, among others.

**National Gallery of Art Sculpture Garden** – *On the Mall at 7th St. & Constitution Ave. NW.* This six-acre urban oasis is filled with trees, flowerbeds and contemporary sculptures by the likes of Alexander Calder, Claes Oldenburg and Joan Miró. In winter, the garden's reflecting pool, with its dramatic circular fountain, doubles as an ice-skating rink *(see Musts for Fun)*.

> ### Micro Visit
>
> A trip to the immense NGA can be daunting, but a few minutes spent at the museum's **Micro Gallery** can help simplify your visit. Located in the art information room *(to the left of the main entrance)*, the Micro Gallery is an interactive computer system that allows visitors to explore more than 1,700 works of art from the museum's permanent collection using touch-screen monitors. Orient yourself to the museum with maps and practical information; survey the life and work of more than 650 artists; view the museum catalog; or create a personal tour of works you want to see, complete with printed maps showing their location.

## Arthur M. Sackler Gallery★★

*The Smithsonian Quadrangle at 1050 Independence Ave. SW. 202-633-4880. www.asia.si.edu Open year-round daily 10am– 5:30pm. Closed Dec 25. An underground gallery links the Sackler to the adjacent Freer Gallery, with which it's closely associated.*

If your tastes run more toward ancient than modern art, then you'll enjoy the Sackler. Dedicated to the study and exhibition of the arts of Asia from the Neolithic period to the present, the Sackler Gallery's major strengths are in Chinese jades and bronzes, ancient Near Eastern gold and silverwork and a collection of 11C–19C Islamic manuscripts. The core of the museum's holdings was a gift from **Dr. Arthur M. Sackler** (1913–1987), the New York psychiatrist, medical researcher and publisher, who donated 1,000 objects from his personal collection to the Smithsonian Institution in 1982.

**Jade Collection** – The mountains of the Chinese provinces contained rich veins of nephrite jade, a gemstone so prized by the Chinese that they associate it with the five cardinal virtues: charity, modesty, courage, justice and wisdom. The Sackler has a jade collection of more than 450 decorated objects dating back to 3000 BC.

**Chinese Bronzes** – The gallery's bronzes date from the Shang through the Han dynasties (1700 BC–AD 220). Many of these objects have lengthy inscriptions, which provide a wealth of information about this period.

**Ancient Near Eastern Gold and Silver** – The civilizations that developed in ancient Iran, Anatolia (present-day Turkey) and the region around the Caucasus Mountains are credited with introducing metalwork as early as 7000 BC. Over the centuries, the craftspeople of these regions made exquisite objects in copper, silver, gold and lead. Many of the gold and silver ceremonial vessels and ornaments in the Sackler collection date from 3000 BC to the 8C AD.

### Chinese Art Unraveled

Ancient Chinese culture placed particular importance on tradition: Laws and customs were passed down through the generations, and ancestor worship was a common practice. This is probably why ancestor figures often decorate ritual bronzes and jades. The economy was largely agricultural, and the elements of nature became a powerful force in ancient Chinese religion. Clouds, rain, wind and stars appear frequently as symbols on vessels and other objects, which the Chinese used to ward off evil spirits and to ask for the protection of their gods.

## Corcoran Gallery ★★

*17th St. & New York Ave. NW.*
*202-639-1700. www.corcoran.org.*
*Open year-round daily 10am–5pm.*
*Closed Tue, Jan 1 & Dec 25. $5.*

**New Digs**

In 2006 the museum is planning to open a striking new 140,000sq ft wing, designed by renowned architect Frank Gehry. The new building will double the existing gallery space and feature the Children's Center for Art and Technology.

Just a hop, skip and a jump from the White House *(one block southwest)* is the largest non-federal art museum in DC. Counting more than 14,000 works in its permanent holdings, the Corcoran's collection of European and American art, as well as its renowned group of 20C American paintings, sculpture and photography are arranged around a skylit two-story atrium.

Self-made man and respected philanthropist, **William Wilson Corcoran** (1798–1888) began constructing a museum to house his private art collection in 1859. That building—now the Renwick Gallery *(see p 49)*—was almost complete when Corcoran halted the project in 1861. A Southern sympathizer, Corcoran found himself unwelcome in Civil War-era Washington, and he left for Europe in 1862. When he returned after the war, Corcoran resumed his museum project. in 1870 he donated his personal collection, the building and grounds, and a $900,000 endowment to be used "for the purpose of encouraging American genius." One of the nation's first major galleries of art, the Corcoran Gallery opened in 1874.

By 1897 the Corcoran's collection had outgrown its original space, and the elegant white-marble Beaux-Arts structure that now houses the museum opened several blocks south of the old building. Above the new museum's entrance is Corcoran's motto: "Dedicated to Art."

In 1925 Sen. William Andrew Clark of Montana gave the Corcoran his noted collection of works by such European masters as Rembrandt, Turner, Corot and Degas. The Clark Bequest also included the **Salon Doré**, an 18C Parisian salon appointed with gilded woodwork, moldings and paneling.

## Four Centuries of Art

Here's a run-down of the major schools of art represented at the Corcoran:

• **French Impressionism** – Renoir, Pissarro, Monet
• **Hudson River school** – Thomas Cole, Frederic Church, Albert Bierstadt
• **African-American art** – Aaron Douglas, Henry O. Tanner, Raymond Saunders
• **Abstract Expressionism** – Hans Hofmann, Mark Rothko, Helen Frankenthaler

# Freer Gallery★★

*Jefferson Dr. at 12th St. SW.*
*202-357-4880. www.asia.si.edu.*
*Open year-round daily 10am–5:30pm.*
*Closed Dec 25. An underground exhi-*
*bition gallery connects the Freer and*
*the Sackler Gallery.*

If Asian art is your thing, the Freer is for you. First of the Smithsonian museums on the Mall devoted exclusively to art, the Freer Gallery possesses an outstanding Asian collection as well as one of the world's largest collections of works by **James McNeill Whistler** (1834–1903). The marble and granite Renaissance-style structure, which incorporates a central courtyard, was officially opened in 1923.

Wealthy railroad-car manufacturer **Charles L. Freer** (1854–1919) became a keen collector of Asian art. From his first purchase of a Japanese fan in 1887, he gradually amassed thousands of objects, many during trips to India and the Orient. He also bought several Whistler prints in 1887, his initial purchase of works by the artist who would become his good friend. In 1904 Freer revealed plans to bequeath a significant portion of his collections to the Smithsonian Institution and to finance the construction of a building to house the art. From that original gift of some 9,000 works, the museum's Asian holdings have grown to over 27,000 objects (Freer requested that his American collection not be expanded).

**Chinese Collection** – These works include ornamental implements of the emperors of the Ming (1368–1644) and Qing (1644–1911) dynasties, and one of the world's finest collections of ancient bronzes.

**Japanese Collection** – Spanning 4,000 years, the collection highlights hanging scrolls, 15C–19C folding screens, ceramics and lacquered wooden boxes (late-16C–19C), and 13C–17C stone and earthenware tea bowls.

### Whistler's Works

Of special interest among the American works are Whistler's "Notes," miniature oils depicting English landscapes c.1882; and "Nocturnes," dramatic paintings of the Thames River at night. The **Peacock Room**★, Whistler's only existing interior design (1876–77), is permanently installed in Gallery 12. An overhaul of English shipping tycoon Frederick Leyland's London dining room, Whistler's design provides a sumptuous gilded setting for Leyland's collection of blue-and-white Chinese porcelain.

## Hillwood Museum and Gardens ★★

*4155 Linnean Ave. NW.*
*Visit by guided tour only;*
*reservations required.*
*202-686-5807.*
*www.hillwoodmuseum.org.*
*Open year-round Tue–Sat*
*9:30m–5pm. Closed Sun, Mon,*
*Jan & major holidays. $10.*

Cereals and czars might sound like an odd combination, but they both played a key role in the life of businesswoman **Marjorie Merriweather Post** (1887–1973). As heiress to the Post cereal fortune, corn flakes helped make Post rich; her money helped buy fine pieces of art that once belonged to Russia's czars. Today you can see Post's remarkable collection of **Russian decorative arts**★★★—the most extensive of its kind outside Russia—in her columned brick mansion that looks down on Rock Creek Park.

In the late 1930s Marjorie Post travelled with her third husband, Joseph E. Davies, to Moscow, where he served as ambassador from 1937–38. The timing was perfect. About that time, the Soviet government began selling art that had been confiscated from the Imperial family, members of the aristocracy and the Russian Orthodox Church during the Revolution of 1917. The treasures Post and her husband collected illustrate more than 200 years of Russian decorative arts, from the reign of Peter the Great (1682–1725) to the days of the last czar, Nicholas II (1868–1918), when jeweler Carl Fabergé created his fabulous Easter eggs for the Russian royal family.

Reopened in fall 2000 after a three-year renovation, Hillwood is filled with 18C and 19C French furnishings that reflect the elegance of the estate during the time Mrs. Post lived there (from 1955 until she died).

**Icon Room**★★ – Contains Post's finest Fabergé pieces, including two (of the more than 50) Imperial Easter eggs and a diamond nuptial crown worn by Alexandra at her 1894 wedding to Nicholas II.

**Dining Room** – Exquisite inlaid-marble Florentine table seats 30 guests.

**French Drawing Room** – Decked out in the ornate Louis XVI style.

**Russian Porcelain Room** – Shows off dinnerware commissioned by Catherine the Great.

### A Gambol on the Grounds

Outside, you can wander wooded paths that connect a host of gardens, including a formal French parterre hedged by boxwoods, a rose garden encircling a monument marking Mrs. Post's grave, and a Japanese-style garden where waterfalls cascade through a series of ponds.

# Hirshhorn Museum ★★

*Independence Ave. at 7th St. NW.*
*202-357-2700. www.hirshhorn.si.edu.*
*Open year-round daily 10am–5:30pm*
*(open until 8pm in summer). Closed*
*Dec 25.*

You'd never guess that this un-adorned concrete "doughnut" (1966, Gordon Bunshaft) on the Mall houses one of the finest collections of modern art in the country. Elevated on four piers, the drum-shaped building wraps around a fountain plaza that extends beneath the raised building. Sculptures here, which range from the realistic to the monumental and abstract, make up the world's most comprehensive collection of 20C works. The Hirshhorn also claims one of the country's most extensive collections of works by celebrated British sculptor **Henry Moore** (1898–1986).

Born in Latvia, **Joseph Hirshhorn** (1899–1981) immigrated to Brooklyn with his widowed mother and 10 siblings when he was six years old. He eventually became a wealthy financier and turned his attention to collecting art. In the mid-1960s, President Johnson and Smithsonian secretary S. Dillon Ripley convinced Hirshhorn to donate his collection of more than 6,000 works to the Smithsonian. In 1966 Congress established the Hirshhorn Museum and Sculpture Garden. In his will, Hirshhorn left another 6,000 works to the museum.

Some 5,000 paintings, 3,000 pieces of sculpture and mixed media and 4,000 works on paper compose the permanent collection, roughly five percent of which is on view in the museum's three levels at any one time.

**Third Floor** – Paintings are grouped by art movements and organized chronologically, beginning with 20C American works (George Bellows, Marsden Hartley, Mark Rothko, Georgia O'Keeffe).

**Second Floor** – Outer-ring galleries here are reserved for temporary exhibits. On the second and third floors, interior galleries feature small sculptural works by the likes of Matisse, Maillol, Rodin, Degas, Picasso and Giacometti.

**First Floor** – Focuses on changing exhibits from the permanent collection.

### Outdoor Sculpture

The plaza on which the building stands was redesigned in 1991 to create outdoor "rooms" for displaying monumental contemporary sculpture, including works by Alexander Calder, Claes Oldenburg and Juan Muñoz.

Smaller figurative works are featured in the sunken and walled Sculpture Garden *(on the Mall between the Washington Monument and the Capitol)*. Here you'll find sculptures by Auguste Rodin, Alexander Calder, Henry Moore and Barbara Hepworth.

## National Archives★★

Constitution Ave.,
between 7th & 9th Sts.
NW. 202-501-5400 or
866-272-6272.
www.archives.gov.
Open year-round
Mon–Sat 8:45am–5pm
(Tue & Thu until 9pm).
Closed Sun & federal
holidays.

Are you hankering to read Commodore Matthew Perry's journals from his historic 19C mission to Japan? Have you always wanted to see Mathew Brady's Civil War photographs or the photo albums of Hitler's mistress, Eva Braun? If so, you've come to the right place.

An imposing Classical Revival building designed by John Russell Pope, the National Archives and Records Administration—as it is officially designated—safeguards 5 billion paper documents, 9 million aerial photographs, 6 million still photographs and 300,000 video, film and sound recordings.

Completed in 1937, the National Archives filled a pressing need for a central fireproof repository of official and historical records. Before this institution was established, each department of the federal government stored its own archival material, and important documents were frequently lost or damaged.

**Rotunda Revisited** – Reopened in September 2003 after an extensive renovation, the Rotunda inspires reverence with its 75ft-high, half-domed space. The centerpiece is a marble dais where the nation's most revered documents are permanently enshrined. Sealed in new cases, the **Charters of Freedom**★★★ consist of the Declaration of Independence, the Constitution and the Bill of Rights. The renovation made it possible to display all four pages of the Constitution for the first time in history. Displayed in a separate case is a 1297 version of England's Magna Carta, on indefinite loan from Texas billionaire Ross Perot.

In fall 2004 the Archives plans to debut its new permanent exhibit, The Public Vaults, as well as a learning center and a 275-seat theater.

### Research Facilities

*Enter from Pennsylvania Ave. Photo ID required. Children under 16 must be accompanied by an adult. 202-501-5400.*

If you're doing scholarly research, head for the ornately paneled **Central Research Room** *(2nd floor)*. Among the holdings here are the papers of the Continental Congress, congressional records and historic correspondence.

If you want to trace your family tree, the **Microfilm Research Room** *(4th floor)* is the place to go. It contains census information, military service records, and ship-passenger arrival lists. Staff members are available on-site to provide information about how to research your family history.

## National Museum of African Art★★

*950 Independence Ave. SW. 202-357-4600. www.nmafa.si.edu. Open year-round daily 10am–5:30pm. Closed Dec 25.*

Come unravel the mystery and magic behind African art at this museum. Devoted to the research, acquisition and display of traditional African arts—especially those of the sub-Saharan regions—the museum owns a permanent collection numbering more than 7,000 items. Originally located in a row of Capitol Hill town houses, the National Museum of African Art now occupies more spacious quarters in the underground Smithsonian Gardens complex on the Mall. Pieces in bronze, copper, wood, ivory and fiber from the permanent collection are rotated among the permanent exhibits here. Throughout the galleries, you'll also find traditional and contemporary African ceramics. Temporary exhibits of African art are arranged from private and public collections, both in the US and abroad.

### Out of Africa

Given the pervasive role of religion in African culture, most objects created for utilitarian, economic, aesthetic or ritual purposes are loaded with religious significance. Unlike most cultures throughout the world, which keep written documents, many African cultures rely on sculptured works and other artifacts to pass down values and beliefs from generation to generation. These objects are generally infused with symbolic meanings. An enlarged head, for example, represents power and wisdom.

**Images of Power and Identity** – Initiation masks, fertility icons, medicinal figurines and other ritual objects are organized by region, emphasizing how geography determines what an object will be made of, as well as its form and style.

**Ancient Benin** – The museum's holdings of art from the ancient West African kingdom of Benin (present-day Nigeria) includes several cast-copper alloy sculptures. Ceremonial figures, heads, pendants and plaques were created between the 15C and 19C and reveal the elaborate rituals and ornate regalia worn by the Benin oba (king) before British colonial rule.

**Art of the Personal Object** – This part of the collection illustrates the beauty and tremendous diversity of design present in everyday objects.

# National Museum of American History ★★

*Constitution Ave., between 12th & 14th Sts. NW. 202-357-2700. www.americanhistory.si.edu. Open year-round daily 10am–5:30pm. Closed Dec 25.*

Where else but at the "nation's attic" can you see such national icons as the Star-Spangled Banner, Archie Bunker's chair and a 1913 Model T Ford? The National Museum of American History's exhibits capture the essence of America's material and social development and explore key events in the nation's past.

Totaling some three million objects, the museum's collection began in 1858, when models from the US Patent Office were transferred to the Smithsonian Institution. The current marble structure opened in 1964 as the National Museum of History and Technology; it was renamed the National Museum of American History in 1980.

**First Floor** – Discover the extent to which agriculture, transportation and power machinery made the "good life" possible in America, and examine the impact and evolution of science and technology.

### Tips For Visiting

To see the American Presidency exhibit, obtain a free timed-entry pass immediately upon arrival at the museum. Passes are available at the 3rd-floor ticket booth, adjacent to the exhibit entrance, or in advance through Ticketmaster *(800-551-7328; handling fee applies)*. The museum is currently undergoing a long-term renovation; some sections may be temporarily relocated, and others may not be on view. Call or check the Web site for information.

**Second Floor** – Displays deal with America as a changing nation. Here you'll find the Star-Spangled Banner Conservation Laboratory. The lab and its companion exhibit, Preserving the Star-Spangled Banner: The Flag That Inspired a Nation, are part of a three-year conservation project to restore the **Star-Spangled Banner**★ that survived British shelling at Fort McHenry in 1814 and inspired America's national anthem. After conservation is complete, the flag will become part of a new exhibit, For Which It Stands: The American Flag in American Life.

**Third Floor** – Exhibits here focus on armed-forces history and the development of money. Outside the entrance to **The American Presidency**★, a jumble of campaign buttons, hats, shirts, posters and other items demonstrates the lengths to which presidential candidates will go to get votes. Inside, 900 objects illustrate the winners' personalities: John Quincy Adams' chess set, Abe Lincoln's top hat, and Bill Clinton's saxophone represent some of the quirkier examples.

# National Museum of Natural History★★

*Constitution Ave. at 10th St. NW. 202-357-2700. www.nmnh.si.edu.*
*Open year-round daily 10am–5:30pm. Closed Dec 25.*

From dinosaur bones to glittering gemstones to a creepy-crawly insect zoo, you'll find something for everyone at this Smithsonian facility, which ranks as one of the most visited museums in the world. Two floors of exhibits and two large-format cinemas explore life on earth through clues nature has left behind—among Ice Age mammal skeletons and prehistoric fossils as well as artifacts of human cultures past and present.

Soon after the completion of the Arts and Industries Building in 1881, more space was needed to accommodate the rapidly expanding Smithsonian collections. In 1903 Congress authorized the construction of the Smithsonian's third building, today known as the National Museum of Natural History. The original four-story granite Classical Revival structure was completed in 1910. Today the expanded 16-acre museum encompasses 300,000sq ft of exhibition space, conserves more than 124 million specimens and provides laboratory facilities for 500 geologists, zoologists, botanists, anthropologists and paleontologists.

**Gem and Mineral Collection**★★★ – The museum's most popular attraction is housed in Geology Hall. Here you'll be dazzled by some of the world's biggest gems (and you thought diamonds were a girl's best friend):

- Hope Diamond, the largest blue diamond in the world at 45.5 carats
- Oppenheimer Diamond (uncut and upolished) at 253.7 carats
- Star of Asia sapphire from Sri Lanka at 330 carats
- Headlight-size golden topaz from Brazil, the largest cut gemstone in the world at 22,892.5 carats
- Hooker Emerald at 75 carats
- Rosser Reeves Ruby at 138.7 carats
- Flawless quarz ball from Burma, measuring 127.88 inches

### Tips For Visiting

Start your visit in the first-floor rotunda, dominated by a 13ft-tall African bush elephant. An information desk to the left of the mall entrance provides a free map and guide. At the rear of the hall is the box office for the IMAX and Immersion theaters. In the Immersion Cinema, audience members can manipulate the onscreen action with their own control panels. Tickets for either theater may be purchased up to two weeks in advance *(call 202-633-7400 or 877-932-4629 for tickets, times and information)*. The museum is undergoing long-term renovation; some exhibits listed may be relocated or not on view.

**Dinosaurs and Fossils** – Kids love dinosaurs, and the ones at the Natural History Museum are no exception. Circling the Dinosaur Hall is a chain of galleries that describe the parade of life from the "Big Bang" 4.6 billion years ago through the Cenozoic era, which continues today.

Some of the dino skeletons here include:

• Triceratops

• 90ft diplodocus

• A life-size model of a pterosaur

• *Tyranosaurus rex*

• *Stegosaurus stenops*

• Casts of bone-headed dinosaurs, or pachycephalosaurs

**African Voices** – This large-scale exhibit uses film clips, recorded narratives, peotry excerpts and music, along with 400 artifacts from the museum's permanent collection, to explore thousands of years of African history.

**Discovery Room** – Touch and examine various objects and artifacts (fossils, minerals, and animals—both living and preserved).

**Insect Zoo** – Kids can easily peer into the low cases here, to see living and preserved insects. As a group, arthropods—which make up 90 percent of animal life on earth—have survived for 475 million years. If you're not an arachnaphobe, take in one of the tarantula feedings *(Tue–Fri 10:30am, 11:30am & 1:30pm; weekend 11:30am, 12:30pm & 1:30pm)*.

## National Portrait Gallery★★

*Old Patent Office Building, 8th & F Sts. NW. 202-357-2700. www.npg.si.edu.*
*Open year-round daily 10am–5:30pm. Closed Dec 25.*

Think of the National Portrait Gallery as America's family album—a huge one that holds 15,000 paintings, sculptures, photographs, engravings and drawings. To be displayed here, portraits must be original works of art and must depict men and women who have made "significant contributions to the history, development and culture" of the US.

The Portrait Gallery occupies the grand **Old Patent Office Building**★★, built in 1867 in the Greek Revival style. It shares this enormous building with the Smithsonian American Art Museum, which it connect to via hallway galleries. If you want a pleasant spot to take a break, head for the interior courtyard, with its cast-iron fountains and monumental sculptures.

**First Floor** – Here you'll find Champions of American Sport (tennis star Arthur Ashe, baseball's Ty Cobb) and popular figures from the Performing Arts (actress Marilyn Monroe, dancer Martha Graham, composer George Gershwin).

### Patently New

Even buildings need a facelift. A $200 million renovation of the Old Patent Office Building began in January 2000 and is expected to take five years. During that time, work will be done on the exterior masonry as well as the interior walls, floors and ceilings. A new two-acre copper roof will be added, and the stained-glass Great Hall skylight will be restored and reinstalled.

**Second Floor** – Portraits are arranged in chronological order beginning with the Founding Fathers and leading to the present. Gilbert Stuart's portrait of George Washington that was used for his likeness on the one-dollar bill is here—it's called the **Lansdowne portrait**★. American presidents, poets (Carl Sandburg, Robert Frost), Native Americans and giants of industry (J.D. Rockefeller, Andrew Carnegie are also on view, along with military leaders like Douglas MacArthur and George C. Marshall.

**Third Floor** – Be sure to see the **Great Hall**, which occupies the south wing. It's decorated with multicolored English tiles, carved ceiling medallions, and a yellow and blue central skylight.

## Phillips Collection★★

*1600 21st St. NW. 202-387-2151. www.phillipscollection.org. Open year-round Tue–Sat 10am–5pm, Thu 10am–8:30pm, Sun noon–5pm. Closed Mon & major holidays. $8 weekends (free weekdays).*

Are the museums on the Mall overwhelming you? Try this charmer, set on a quiet corner a few short blocks from bustling Dupont Circle. A small museum of great distinction, the Phillips Collection is the nation's first museum of modern art. Here you'll see outstanding works by prominent American and European artists in an intimate house setting.

The grandson of one of the cofounders of the Jones and Laughlin Steel Co., **Duncan Phillips** (1886–1966) founded this gallery in 1921 in his family's unpre-

## Sunday At The Phillips

If you've got a Sunday afternoon to spare, why not spend it at the Phillips Collection? After you've had your fill of fabulous artwork, you can relax and listen to up-and-coming musical talent from around the world at the Sunday Concert series *(free with museum admission)*. An institution since 1941, Sunday concerts are held from September to May at 5pm in the oak-paneled Music Room. There are no reserved seats, so get there early.

tentious brick and brownstone home as a memorial to his father and his brother, James.

Phillips and his wife, Marjorie Acker, a talented painter in her own right, expanded the collection, which now contains some 2,500 works and includes all the major French Impressionists, post-Impressionists, Cubists and 17C and 18C masters (Goya, El Greco, Chardin).

## Phillips Picks

**Luncheon of the Boating Party** – On exhibit in a second-floor gallery is the museum's most renowned treasure, painted by **Pierre Auguste Renoir** (1841–1919) in 1881. Phillips and his wife purchased this work in 1923, for the record sum of $125,000.

**Paul Klee** – The second floor contains a room devoted exclusively to the delightful works of the renowned Swiss painter (1879–1940).

**Bonnard Collection** – Reputed to be the country's largest collection of paintings by French artist **Pierre Bonnard** (1867–1947), this group of works is housed in the adjoining Goh Annex.

**Mark Rothko** – A small gallery on the first floor displays four important Abstract Expressionist works by Rothko (1903–1970) who is known for his hauntingly simple canvases filled with large expanses of color.

# United States Holocaust Memorial Museum★★

*South of Independence Ave., between 14th St. & Raoul Wallenberg Pl. SW. 202-488-0406. www.ushmm.org. Open year-round daily 10am–5:30pm. Closed Yom Kippur & Dec 25.*

A deeply moving history lesson awaits you at this large museum/research complex, conceived to tell the tragic story of the Nazi extermination of millions of Jews and others during World War II. Located adjacent to the Bureau of Engraving and Printing, the striking five-story brick and limestone building (1993, I.M. Pei & Partners) is designed as a post-Modern "penitentiary," with "watchtowers" lining the north and south walls. Exposed metal beams and metal-framed glass doors of the Hall of Witness, the building's 7,500sq ft glass-roofed central atrium, amplify the feeling of imprisonment.

**Fourth Floor** – The compelling permanent exhibit begins on the fourth floor. Before entering the elevator, you'll receive a keepsake photo identification card detailing the background and fate of a particular Holocaust victim. In darkened surroundings, you're confronted with photographs, films and artifacts. Informative panels tell the horrific story of the deprivation of property, human rights and eventually the lives of nearly six million European Jews and five million others.

**Third Floor** – Concentration-camp life is evoked on the third floor. Personal articles, food bowls and work implements are interspersed with an actual railcar and a scale model of a gas chamber. Especially sensitive topics are presented discreetly, for optional viewing, on sunken video monitors.

**Second Floor** – Exhibits here hail the valor and success of rescue and resistance efforts. Film footage recording the liberating armies' arrival at the camps is continually shown. One display focuses on **Raoul Wallenberg**, the Swedish diplomat stationed in Budapest who led the War Refuge Board's mission to save Hungarian Jews. At the end of your visit, you might want to spend some quiet time inside the 60ft high Hall of Remembrance, an unadorned, light-filled space for contemplation and commemorative ceremonies.

---

### Tips For Visiting

Timed passes, available at the box office, are required for entrance to the permanent exhibit. Advance passes can be obtained from Tickets.com *(800-400-9373; service charge applies)*.

Instead of viewing the intense permanent exhibit, children can see the special exhibit entitled **Daniel's Story: Remember the Children**.

---

## City Museum of DC ★

*801 K St. NW.*
*202-383-1800.*
*www.citymuseumdc.org.*
*Open year-round Tue–Sun*
*10am–5pm. Closed Mon &*
*major holidays. $3.*

Finally, there's a museum that tells the story of America's capital city. Opened in spring 2003 by the Historical Society of Washington, DC, the City Museum occupies the former Beaux-Arts-style Carnegie Library (1903) in Mount Vernon Square. The museum personalizes the city's history through first-hand accounts of events told by some of the people who have lived in Washington over the years.

### Digging Up History

Bring the kids and uncover DC history for yourself at the City Museum's ground-floor **Archaeology Lab**. Archaeological kits available at the lab will challenge visitors to do some detective work relating to a specific site by examining archaeological clues from digs around the city. Call the museum to check lab hours.

Begin your visit in the first-floor main gallery *(west wing)*, where you'll find **Washington Perspectives**, a giant glass-block floor map composed of 1,000 aerial photographs of the city, marvelously detailed with all its neighborhoods and monuments. Around it, four facades each explore a different period of the capital's history (1790–present) through photos, video clips and artifacts. Be sure to see the 15-minute **multimedia presentation** in the east-wing theater, for a trip back into DC's past, complete with special effects. Researchers will find a wealth of information about the city in the state-of-the art **library** on the second floor.

### Changing Exhibits

**First Floor** – Exhibits in the **Community Galleries** highlight some of DC's 125 culturally diverse neighborhhoods.

**Second Floor** – The **Collections Gallery** hosts exhibits that highlight DC-based collections of prints, photos and paintings of the capital. Displays in the **Changing Exhibits Gallery** rotate thematic selections from the Society's holdings of some 14,000 books and pamphlets, 100,000 photos, 300 maps and 5,000 objects relating to the capital's history.

## International Spy Museum ★

*800 F St. NW. at 8th St.*
*202-393-7798.*
*www.spymuseum.org.*
*Open Apr–Oct 10am–8pm,*
*Nov–Mar 10am–6pm. Closed*
*Jan 1, Thanksgiving Day & Dec*
*25. $13.*

All is not what it seems. And nowhere is this more evident than at the International Spy Museum. If you've ever wondered what it would be like to be a secret agent, here's your chance to adopt a cover identity and learn some of the tricks of this shadowy trade. (They can't give away all the secrets, though—some of them are classified!)

Located across the street from the National Portrait Gallery, the Spy Museum opened in July 2002 in a complex of five historic buildings dating from 1872 to 1892. Your adventure begins on the third floor, where you'll be assigned a cover identity and confronted with the real world of spying in the **Briefing Film**. Then it's on to the **School for Spies**, to examine gadgets from buttonhole cameras to lipstick pistols and test your skills to see if you're cut out to be a secret agent. In the museum's gift shops, you can pick up your own disguise or even purchase spy collectibles that were actually used in the field.

**The Secret History of History** – Trace spying from George Washington's era to the beginnings of the secret service in this behind-the-scenes exhibit.

**Spies Among Us** – Discover real-life spy stories from World War II.

**War of the Spies** – Look behind the Iron Curtain during the Cold War and see how spy technology developed from Maxwell Smart's shoe phone to sophisticated spy satellites.

**21st Century** – Face the challenges that the intelligence community deals with today.

### Eating Undercover

Need to grab a quick bite between missions? Try the **Spy City Café** for fresh sandwiches, soups, pizzas and salads, served cafeteria-style. While you eat, plan your next caper using the tabletop maps of DC spy sites. If you prefer a private place for that secret rendez-vous, **Zola** fills the bill. You'll be well concealed here in sleek red velvet booths, which feature spy ovals cut into them so you can into them so you can make sure you're not being followed. One-way mirrors in the booths let you monitor activity in the kitchen, where the chef whips up acclaimed New American cuisine. Both restaurants are located in the museum complex.

# Kreeger Museum ★

*2401 Foxhall Rd. NW. Visit by guided tour only year-round Mon–Fri 10:30am, 1:30pm, Sat 10:30am & 2pm. Reservations required. 202-337-3050. www.kreegermuseum.org. Closed Sun, Mon, Aug & major holidays. $8.*

It's worth a short drive northwest of Georgetown to visit the Kreeger. Hidden behind a high wall on 5.5 wooded acres in a well-to-do neighborhood, this post-Modern mansion contains the wonderful art holdings of former residents **David and Carmen Kreeger**. Their 200-piece collection includes 19C and 20C European paintings by renowned artists as well as African and 20C art.

A resident of Washington since the 1930s, Kreeger made his fortune in the insurance industry, and he and his wife both dabbled in art and music. To house their growing art collection, Kreeger hired architect Philip Johnson in the late 1960s to build a house that could function as a museum and performance venue. After her husband's death in 1990, Mrs. Kreeger vacated the house. In 1994 it opened to the public as a museum.

Designed as a concert hall and gallery, the **Great Hall** provides ample space for hanging art on its carpeted walls. The hall, lit by floor-to-ceiling windows at each end, opens onto a marble terrace—a dramatic setting for outdoor sculpture by Henry Moore, Jacques Lipchitz and Isamu Noguchi.

- **Great Hall** – Paintings and small sculptural works.
- **Dining Room** – French Impressionist paintings, including nine works by Monet.
- **Library** – Works by Corot and Mondrian.
- **Stair Landing** – Modern paintings by Picasso, Miró and Man Ray.
- **Lower Level** – Large acrylic works representative of Abstract Expressionism and Color Field painting; African art, primarily large wooden masks.

### For Love Or Money

Kreeger began collecting art, not as an investment, but "for love." He and his wife searched out pieces that appealed to them personally, without a thought for what the art might be worth at some point in the future. So the Kreeger collection is truly personal to the couple, who agreed on every piece they purchased. As Kreeger maintained, "art that embodies the creative spirit of men transcends the value of money."

# National Museum of Women in the Arts★

*1250 New York Ave. at 13th St. NW. 202-783-5000. www.nmwa.org. Open year-round Mon–Sat 10am–5pm, Sun noon–5pm. Closed Jan 1, Thanksgiving Day & Dec 25. $5.*

You won't find artwork by any men here. Behind this Beaux-Arts exterior is the world's only major museum devoted exclusively to the works of women artists. Devoting itself to recognizing the achievements of women artists of all periods and nationalities, the National Museum of Women in the Arts maintains a 3,000-piece permanent collection that spans the years from the 16C to the present and covers every medium from native American pottery to abstract sculpture.

Local philanthropists Wilhelmina and Wallace Holladay founded the museum in 1981 as a private institution "to encourage greater awareness of women in the arts and their contributions to the history of art." The Holladays donated their own collection to form the core of the museum's holdings, which today comprises works by more than 800 women artists.

In 1983 the museum purchased its present building from the fraternal order of Masons and transformed the interior into three levels of exhibit space, a library and research center, and a 200-seat auditorium, where public lectures, films and concerts are held. Works from the permanent collection are displayed in the two-story marble **Great Hall** and on the mezzanine; the second and third floors are reserved for temporary exhibits.

## A Sampling of Superlatives

**Oldest Work** – The museum's oldest painting is *Portrait of a Noblewoman* (c.1580) by Lavinia Fontana, a 16C Italian painter from Bologna who is considered the first professional woman artist.

**19C Paintings** – *Sheep by the Sea* (1865) by Rosa Bonheur; *Lady with a Bowl of Violets* (c.1910), by Lilla Cabot Perry, who introduced Monet's work to Americans; *The Bath* (1891), from a renowned series of graphics by American Impressionist Mary Cassatt.

**19C Sculpture** – A rare medium for female artists of that period, 19C sculpture includes pieces by Camille Claudel, Malvina Hoffman and Bessie Potter Vonnoh.

**20C Paintings** – *Alligator Pears in a Basket* (1921) by Georgia O'Keeffe; *Self-Portrait Dedicated to Leon Trotsky* (1937) by Mexican artist Frida Kahlo; *Singing Their Songs* (1992) by African-American painter Elizabeth Catlett.

## Renwick Gallery ★

*Pennsylvania Ave. & 17th St. NW.*
*202-357-2700. www.americanart.si.edu.*
*Open year-round daily 10am–5:30pm.*
*Closed Dec 25.*

If your only exposure to American arts and crafts has been at seasonal local craft fairs, you'll be surprised at the high quality of contemporary and traditional American craftsmanship displayed here. From striking contemporary quilts to delicate art glass to fanciful hand-wrought iron gates, the variety of the Renwick's collection will amaze you.

Located just across the street from the White House, the Second Empire-style gem is named for its architect, William Renwick Jr. (whose claims to fame include the Smithsonian Castle and Saint Patrick's Cathedral in New York City). This was the original home of the **Corcoran Gallery** *(see p 33)*, commissioned in 1858 by financier William Wilson Corcoran. With its distinctive mansard roof, the lovely redbrick building is decorated with square sandstone columns and garlands.

The Renwick's permanent collection is displayed on the second floor. Here you'll outstanding 20C crafts, ranging from traditional basketry to abstract works in glass, wood, clay, metal and fiber. First-floor galleries focus on temporary exhibits.

**Grand Salon** – Designed as a "hall of paintings," the 4,300sq ft room soars to a height of 40ft. Paintings from the Smithsonian American Art Museum *(currently closed for renovation)* hang in tiers on the raspberry-colored walls.

**Octagon Room** – The smaller Victorian gallery opposite the Grand Salon showcases works by Winslow Homer, Albert Pinkham Ryder and Thomas Wilmer Dewing.

### Jackie Saves The Day

In 1874 the Corcoran Gallery of Art, as the building was then called, opened as Washington's first art museum. By 1897, the collection had grown too large for its original digs and William Corcoran built the present-day Corcoran Museum to house his treasures.

Sold to the government for $300,000, the old building was used by the US Court of Claims until 1964, the year demolition was proposed. Former First Lady Jacqueline Kennedy led the campaign to preserve the landmark, and in 1965 President Lyndon Johnson turned the building over to the Smithsonian as a gallery of "art, crafts and design." Restored to its original appearance (the splendid Grand Salon had been turned into office space when the Court occupied it), the refurbished Renwick opened as a department of the Smithsonian American Art Museum in 1972.

# Smithsonian American Art Museum ★

*Old Patent Office Building, 8th & G Sts. NW. The museum will be closed for renovation until summer 2006. Entrance on G St. 202-357-2700. www.nmaa.si.edu.*

Sure, Europe claims more than its share of fine art, but don't overlook the US. The Smithsonian American Art Museum is the country's only museum dedicated to art and artists of the United States. Containing nearly 40,000 works by 7,000 American artists, the permanent collection spans 300 years, from Colonial quilts to American Impressionist paintings to 21C art glass.

Located in the landmark Old Patent Office Building, this museum contains the country's oldest federal collection of art, which began when Washingtonian John Varden donated his collection of artwork to the federal government in 1841. In 1862 that collection was transferred to the Smithsonian Institution, and eventually ended up in the Old Patent Office Building. Named the National Museum of American Art (NMAA) in 1980, the facility was renamed the Smithsonian American Art Museum in 2000 to better reflect its mission of displaying exclusively the works of US artists. The renovation, which began in 2001, will add a new roof and additional gallery space, among other features.

> **On The Road**
>
> While the museum is being renovated, parts of the collection are touring the US. The museum has assembled hundreds of rarely seen works into five thematic exhibits, ranging from photographs to paintings by African-American masters. These exhibits will tour 30 cities in 20 states through 2005. Watch your local papers or check the museum's Web site—highlights from the Smithsonian American Art Museum may be coming soon to a venue near you.

## Touring Exhibits

**African American Masters** – Highlights 61 works by the likes of Richmond Barthé, Romare Bearden and William H. Johnson incorporate social influences such as politics, spirituality, music and folkore.

**The Land Through A Lens** – Photographs by Ansel Adams, Timothy O'Sullivan, Aaron Siskind and others capture the beauty and symbolism of America's land.

**Graphic Masters** – Works on paper from the 1860s to the 1990s spotlight watercolors, drawings and pastels by a host of American artists.

**Masters of Their Craft** – Showcases pieces in clay, fiber, glass, metal and wood, including glass sculptures by Dale Chihuly.

**Calico and Chintz** – The 22 extraordinary quilts in this exhibit were made in America before 1850.

## National Building Museum

*401 F. St. NW, between 4th & 5th Sts. 202-272-2448. www.nbm.org. Open year-round Mon–Sat 10am–5pm, Sun 11am–5pm. Closed Jan 1, Thanksgiving Day & Dec 25.*

Here's a building devoted to buildings. Yes, you read that right. The National Building Museum celebrates America's achievement in the building arts. Housed in the 1887 **Pension Building**★, the museum's exhibits demystify the building process and show changing architectural styles and construction techniques. To this end, the permanent collection claims 40,000 photographs, 68,000 prints and drawings, and 2,100 objects, including architectural elements and samples of building materials. Exhibits, which change frequently, are arranged around a vast interior court known as the **Great Hall**. Measuring 316ft long by 116ft wide, the Great Hall is lined with eight 75ft Corinthian columns painted to look like marble.

### Long-term Exhibits

**Washington: Symbol and City** – Looks at DC both as a federal city and as a place where people live and work.

**Tools As Art: The Hechinger Collection** – Kids will like this one, which showcases fish made out of visegrips and bird sculptures fashioned from saws, among other whimsical works of art.

## Old Post Office

*Pennsylvania Ave. & 12th St. NW. 202-606-8691. www.oldpostofficedc.com. Open Jun–Labor Day Mon–Fri 9am–7:45pm, weekends 10am–5:45pm. Rest of the year Mon–Fri 9am–4:45pm, weekends 10am–5:45pm. Closed Jan 1, Thanksgiving Day & Dec 25.*

This Pennsylvania Avenue landmark is lucky to still be around. When it was completed in 1899 as the headquarters of the US Postal Service, many people didn't like the way it looked. The massive granite Post Office, with its rough-faced masonry and corner turrets, was nicknamed "Old Tooth" for the 315ft tower that stuck out above the rest of the structure. Designed in the Richardsonian Romanesque style, the Post Office didn't match the Neoclassical architecture that was popular in DC at the time. It was saved from the wrecker's ball at the eleventh hour and converted into a multifunctional complex with office and commercial space. Today the **Old Post Office Pavilion** festival market attracts residents and tourists alike throughout the year.

**Pavilion** – The first three levels of the central glass-roofed **courtyard** teem with shops, restaurants, a food court, and a stage for live entertainment.

**Tower** – From the observation deck at the top of the clock tower you'll have a great **view** of DC *(take the glass elevator from the courtyard)*. Near the summit are the 10 **Congress bells** that are played to mark the opening and closing sessions of Congress.

The section of the Mall west of 15th Street is the setting for the nation's most revered monuments. Roughly ringing the Tidal Basin—whose banks are justly famous for the flowering Japanese cherry trees that burst with delicate pink blossoms in early spring—the memorials honor some of the greatest and most heroic Americans. A memorial commemorating World War II veterans will be added to the Mall in 2004.

## Franklin Delano Roosevelt Memorial★★★

*Tidal Basin, west of the Jefferson Memorial. 202-426-6841.*
*www.nps.gov/frde. Open year-round 24 hours daily. Closed Dec 25.*

Set along the famous **Cherry Tree Walk** bordering the Tidal Basin, this memorial to the nation's 32nd president brings to life the four terms of office held by Franklin D. Roosevelt. Ornamental plantings, waterfalls and quiet pools create a feeling of tranquility at the expansive memorial, which opened in May 1997.

Born to wealthy parents in New York, Franklin Roosevelt (1882–1945) graduated from Harvard University and Columbia University Law School. He entered politics in 1910 when he was elected to the New York Senate. As president, FDR led the nation through some of the most difficult periods in its history—the Great Depression and World War II. Through his radio fireside chats, Roosevelt inspired optimism and courage in the American people. Today his words still reach out to us from the walls of his memorial.

Four outdoor galleries of red South Dakota granite contain sculptured figures and cascading water walls designed to symbolize each of FDR's terms as president:

**First-Term Room** (1933–37) focuses on the president's determination to overcome the nation's economic problems.

**Second-Term Room** (1937–41) represents the US in the depths of the Great Depression.

**Third Term Room** (1941–45) uses a jumbled landscape of jagged granite blocks to symbolize the devastation caused by World War II.

**Fourth-Term Room** (1945) depicts the president's death. A statue of Eleanor Roosevelt commemorates her role as First Lady and first delegate to the United Nations.

### Commemorating A Courageous Spirit

In January 2001 President Bill Clinton dedicated an addition to the FDR memorial. Located at the site's entrance, a bronze statue sculpted by Robert Graham depicts FDR sitting in the wheelchair he used daily after polio crippled him in 1921. Although the idea of illustrating FDR in his wheelchair met with great controversy, officials eventually decided that the statue emphasized Roosevelt's indomitable spirit.

## Jefferson Memorial★★★

*Ohio Dr., on the south bank of the Tidal Basin. 202-246-6841. www.nps.gov/thje. Open year-round daily 8am–midnight. Closed Dec 25.*

You might think that the south bank of the Tidal Basin is a strange place for the Roman Pantheon. No, your eyes aren't playing tricks on you—this is a 20C adaptation, designed by John Russell Pope in 1936 to pay homage to the nation's third president, Thomas Jefferson (1801–09).

Opened to the public in 1942, the white marble monument echoes the Classical style of architecture that Jefferson reproduced at Monticello, his Virginia home *(see Excursions)*. Visitors enter through a columned entrance portico that rises from a wide paved plaza. Before you go in, look up to the front of the pediment, where sculpted images show Jefferson surrounded by the four other members of the committee chosen to draft the Declaration of Independence: Benjamin Franklin, John Adams, Roger Sherman and Robert Livingston. Inside the memorial's open-air interior stands an imposing 19ft-tall bronze statue of a middle-aged Thomas Jefferson, by sculptor Rudolph Evans. Jefferson's likeness clutches a rolled parchment on which the Declaration of Independence is written.

### A Man For All Seasons

**Thomas Jefferson** (1743–1826) was a true Renaissance man. In addition to being a skilled statesman, Jefferson was equally celebrated as an architect (he designed Monticello and the University of Virginia), a philosopher, a horticulturist, a musician and an inventor. A native Virginian, Jefferson studied law at the College of William and Mary, and served with George Washington in the House of Burgesses. In 1774 Jefferson was elected to the first Continental Congress in Philadelphia. At the second Continental Congress a year later, he was appointed to a committee charged with drafting a statement to the British Crown that justified the colonists' stand on independence. Noted for his eloquent writings, Jefferson was encouraged to draft the document himself. On July 4, 1776, the **Declaration of Independence** was signed by the Continental Congress.

Jefferson served as vice president under John Adams before being elected the nation's third president in 1801. During his two terms in office, the US negotiated the Louisiana Purchase with France, which doubled the size of the young country and opened the way west. In 1809 Jefferson retired to his home at Monticello near Charlottesville, Virginia.

## Korean War Veterans Memorial★★★

*Independence Ave. at French Dr. SW. 202-426-6841. www.nps.gov/kowa. Open year-round daily 8am–11:45pm. Closed Dec 25.*

The first thing you see as you approach the Korean War Veterans Memorial is a "field" dotted with 19 larger-than-life stainless-steel statues (each about 7ft tall) of men in patrol formation wearing combat rain gear. One side of the field is lined with a 164ft-long wall of polished black granite, sandblasted with the faces of more than 2,500 servicemen and women. Although they are not identified, these faces were taken from actual photographs of people who participated in the Korean conflict. Mounted in the granite, an American flag waves over the inscription: "Our nation honors her sons and daughters who answered the call to defend a country they never knew and a people they never met."

The rim of the circular **Pool of Remembrance**, located behind the flagpole, is etched with the statistics of the lives that were sacrificed in this conflict. Of the 1.5 million Americans who served in the Korean War, more than 54,000 died, some 110,000 were captured or wounded and 8,000 were declared missing.

### "The Forgotten War"

American veterans of the Korean War (1950–1953) attached this nickname to a war they felt was overshadowed by the magnitude of World War II and the controversy of Vietnam. As memories of Korea faded from the national consciousness, veterans began pursuing a means to formally commemorate the war. In 1986 Congress authorized the American Battle Monuments Commission to oversee the design of a memorial. A team of architects from Pennsyl- vania State University won the design competition in 1989 but later withdrew from the project. The Washington, DC firm Cooper-Lecky Architects completed the memorial. Stainless-steel statues were sculpted by Frank Gaylord and the granite mural of faces was crafted by Louis Nelson. At the groundbreaking ceremony in 1992, President George H. Bush stated that the memorial's realization would assure that "no American will ever forget the test of freedom" faced by US troops. The memorial was dedicated in July 1995 by President Bill Clinton and Kim Young Sam, president of the Republic of Korea, on the 42nd anniversary of the war's armistice.

## Lincoln Memorial★★★

*The Mall at 23rd St. NW.
202-426-6841. www.nps.gov/linc.
Open year-round daily 8am–
11:45pm. Closed Dec 25.*

Reproduced on the copper penny and the $5 bill, the facade of the Lincoln Memorial is easy to identify. Architect Henry Bacon designed his version of a Greek temple as a tribute to the nation's 16th president (1861–65). Thirty-six Doric columns—symbolizing the 36 states in the Union at the time of Lincoln's death—form a continuous ring around the monument (states' names are inscribed above the columns). In 1922 the Lincoln Memorial was dedicated in a ceremony attended by Robert Todd Lincoln, the president's only surviving son.

From its stately perch atop a long flight of stairs, the famous marble image of a seated, brooding Lincoln stares out across the city. Renowned 19C sculptor Daniel Chester French created this powerful, 19ft-high marble **statue★★★** that captures Lincoln's strength. The left wall of the memorial is inscribed with Lincoln's celebrated Gettysburg Address (1863).

Stop at the top of the memorial's steps to take in the grand **view★★** of the Mall from the **Reflecting Pool,** which stretches 350ft beyond the Lincoln Memorial, to the Washington Monument.

### Honest Abe

Born in Kentucky in 1809 to a poor farming family, Abraham Lincoln (1809–1865) was a self-educated man. The down-home statesman known as "Honest Abe," is remembered as the Great Emancipator who freed the country from the shackles of slavery. The month after his inauguration as president in March 1861, the first shots of the Civil War were fired at Fort Sumter. For the next four years, the president waged a war to reunite the nation.

In 1863 Lincoln issued the Emancipation Proclamation. More a symbolic gesture than a real reversal of slavery, the proclamation nonetheless set the stage for the passage of the 13th Amendment to the Constitution in 1865, which finally did abolish slavery.

In April 1865, at the start of Lincoln's second term, the long war ended. The president then turned his thoughts to the reconstruction of the South, but his plans were never realized. On April 14, 1865, Lincoln was shot at Ford's Theatre by actor John Wilkes Booth *(see Historic Sites).* The following day, at age 56, President Abraham Lincoln died of his wounds.

## Vietnam Veterans Memorial★★★

*Bacon Dr. & Constitution Ave. NW. 202-426-6841. www.nps.gov/vive. Open year-round daily 8am–11:45pm. Closed Dec 25. Directories specifying the memorial panels on which names appear are located at the approaches to the Wall.*

Known simply as "the Wall," the Vietnam Veterans Memorial is tucked away in the sylvan setting of Constitution Gardens. Though it was conceived in controversy, this solemn black-granite wall has become one of America's most cherished and moving shrines—a place of healing where family and friends can touch the names of loved ones lost in battle.

Inset in a low hill, the 493.5ft-long memorial is actually made up of two triangular panels that join at a 125-degree angle. The two arms of the wall point toward the Washington Monument and the Lincoln Memorial. Their polished surfaces are inscribed with the names of 58,226 men and women killed or missing in the Vietnam War. Beginning with the first casualty in 1959 and ending in 1975, the names are arranged chronologically, according to when each died or was declared missing. Those who died in the war have diamonds next to their names; those missing in action or imprisoned are indicated by a cross.

**Vietnam Women's Memorial** – In a grove of trees just south of the Wall stands a bronze statue (1992, Glenna Goodacre) of three military women tending a wounded soldier; it is dedicated to the more than 265,000 women who served in Vietnam.

### "Serenity, Without Conflict"

The idea for this monument came from a small group of Vietnam veterans living in the capital. Troubled by the public's indifference toward those Americans who served in the Southeast Asian conflict, they formed the Vietnam Veterans Memorial Fund in 1979 to solicit congressional support and to set up fundraising efforts. In 1980, President Jimmy Carter signed a resolution authorizing the creation of the monument. The Wall was dedicated in November 1982.

The national design competition for the memorial attracted 1,421 entries. The winning design was submitted by Maya Ying Lin, a 21-year-old architectural student at Yale University. Lin's wall was conceived as a symbol of healing. As she explained, "Take a knife and cut open the earth, and with time the grass would heal it."

## The Washington Monument★★★

*On the Mall at 15th St. Timed admission tickets are required. Free same-day tickets are available from the kiosk at 15th St. & Madison Dr. 202-246-6841. www.nps.gov/wamo. Open year-round daily 9am–4:45pm. Advance reservations ($2 fee) can be made by calling 800-967-2283 or online at www.reservations.nps.gov. Closed Dec 25.*

This 555ft-tall white marble obelisk is hard to miss. It's the capital's most conspicuous landmark as well as the world's tallest freestanding stone structure. A tribute to America's first president, George Washington (1789–97), the Washington Monument is also an icon of the city that bears his name. Prominent architect Robert Mills designed the shaft, whose cornerstone was laid on July 4, 1848. Construction proceeded slowly, with ever-insufficient funds finally running dry in 1853. The unfinished obelisk sat neglected until President Ulysses S. Grant authorized its completion 25 years later. In 1888 the Washington Monument officially opened to the public. Take the elevator up to the top, where small windows afford great panoramic **views★★★** of the city.

| Washington Monument Statistics | | | |
|---|---|---|---|
| **Height**: | 555ft 5 1/8in | **Weight**: | 90,854 tons |
| **Thickness at base**: | 15ft | **Thickness at top**: | 18in |
| **Width at base**: | 55ft 1 1/2in | **Width at top**: | 34ft 5 1/2in |
| **Depth of foundation**: | 36ft 10in | **Cost**: | $1,187,710 |

### Just George

Soldier and statesman, **George Washington** (1732–1799) began his long military service while in his early 20s, distinguishing himself as a commander during the French and Indian War in the 1750s. A member of the Virginia House of Burgesses in Williamsburg, Virginia after the war, Washington became increasingly disenchanted with Britain as resentment over British taxation grew among the colonists. In 1774 he served as one of seven Virginia delegates to the Continental Congress in Philadelphia. A year later, at the second Continental Congress, he was unanimously elected commander of the Continental Army. After his victory against Lord Cornwallis on October 19, 1781, Washington enjoyed a respite from public life at his Virginia plantation, Mount Vernon *(see Nearby Northern Virginia)*. In 1787, when lack of centralized government threatened the new confederation of states, he presided over the Constitutional Congress in Philadelphia. Two years later, the new electoral college unanimously voted Washington the first president of the new nation. After two terms, he refused a third and in 1797 Washington returned for a final time to Mount Vernon.

**G**eorge Washington may not have slept in these venerable landmarks, but that doesn't make this selection of DC historic sights any less important.

# Dumbarton Oaks★★

*1703 32nd St. NW.*
*202-339-6401.*
*www.doaks.org. Open year-round Tue–Sun 2pm–5pm. Closed Mon & major holidays. Gardens open mid-Mar–Oct daily 2pm–6pm. Rest of the year daily 2pm–5pm. $5 (mid-Mar–Oct).*

If you think Dumbarton Oaks is just another house museum, you're in for a surprise. Inside the walls of this early-19C residence, you'll find a fabulous collection of Byzantine and pre-Columbian art. In 1920 Robert and Mildred Bliss purchased the estate, restored it to the Federal style and hired renowned landscape gardener Beatrix Farrand to design extensive gardens. Although Robert Bliss' career in the foreign service prevented the couple from living here until 1933, while they were abroad the couple began collecting Byzantine artifacts. When they returned, they added two pavilions and an enclosed courtyard to display their collection as a public museum. In 1940 the Blisses gave the house, gardens and their Byzantine collection to Harvard University, which still maintains the estate as a research institution and museum.

**Byzantine Collection★★** – More than 1,500 artifacts represent the Byzantine period (4C–15C). These items range from 11C illuminated manuscripts to the collection of 12,000 **Byzantine coins,** one of the most extensive in the world.

**Pre-Columbian Collection★** – Formerly housed in the National Gallery of Art, the Bliss' remarkable collection of objects from Mexico, Central American and South America date back as far as Mexico's Olmec culture (1200 BC).

**Gardens★★** – *Entrance at 31st & R Sts. NW.* Ten acres of formal gardens de-signed by Beatrix Farrand surround Dumbarton Oaks. Added in the 1960s, the graceful **Pebble Garden** is a shallow pool framed by curving borders of velvety moss. The bed of the pool is paved with a mosaic of Mexican stones.

### Conversations Of Consequence

With its 16C stone chimney piece and antique European furnishings, the lovely **Music Room★** was added to the house in 1929. The walls are decorated with tapestries and priceless paintings, including *The Visitation* (c.1610) by El Greco. No less than Russian composer Igor Stravinsky played the grand piano here. But the room is perhaps most noteworthy for hosting delegates from the US, the Soviet Union, China and the United Kingdom in 1944. These meetings, now known as the "Dumbarton Oaks Conversations," helped lay the groundwork for the founding of the United Nations.

## Washington National Cathedral★★

*Massachusetts & Wisconsin Aves. NW. 202-537-6200. www.cathedral.org/cathedral. Open Mon–Fri 10am–5:30pm, Sat 10am–4:30pm, Sun 8am–6:30pm.*

Washington, DC is proud to claim the second-largest cathedral in the US (St. John the Divine in New York City is the largest) and the sixth-largest cathedral in the world. Officially named the Cathedral Church of Saint Peter and Saint Paul, the Gothic-style National Cathedral (as it's popularly known) overlooks the city from its 57-acre perch atop Mount St. Alban.

The inspiration for a national cathedral dates back to Pierre L'Enfant's grand plan for the capital. Although L'Enfant proposed "a great church for national purposes," the idea won little support at first, since the new nation was committed to the separation of church and state. Finally in 1893 Congress authorized the charter of the Protestant Episcopal Cathedral Foundation. Under the leadership of the Right Reverend Dr. Yates Satterlee, first Episcopal bishop of Washington, the foundation purchased the Mount St. Alban site at the turn of the 19C. Bishop Satterlee envisioned a Gothic cathedral that would welcome all, regardless of faith or nationality. In a ceremony held on September 29, 1990—exactly 83 years to the day after the foundation was laid—the final stone was set in place on the St. Paul Tower (south side of the main facade).

### Can You Find Darth Vader?

Before the National Cathedral was completed, a contest was held to challenge children to design a sculpture to decorate the exterior of the building. The third-place winner proposed a statue of *Star Wars* villain Darth Vader. If you look with binoculars, you'll see Darth's head high up on the northwest tower.

### Cool Facts About The Cathedral

- Designed to carry rainwater away from the walls, 110 gargoyles and grotesques decorate the flying buttresses that support the vaulting of the nave.

- The cathedral's nave is 10 stories high and approximately 565ft long.

- The centerpiece of the Indiana limestone facade is the 26ft **rose window**—an abstract composition of 10,500 pieces of colored glass by stained-glass artist Rowan LeCompte.

- Reverend Dr. Martin Luther King Jr. delivered his last Sunday sermon here on March 31, 1968.

- Among the notable Americans interred in the vast underground **crypt** are Helen Keller, her teacher Anne Sullivan, and President Woodrow Wilson.

# Decatur House★

*748 Jackson Pl. NW. 202-842-0920. www.decaturhouse.org. Open year-round Tue–Sat 10am–5pm (Thu until 8pm), Sun noon–5pm. Closed Jan 1, Thanksgiving Day & Dec 25.*

You'd never guess by looking at this sedate 1818 brick town house that the residence saw some pretty lavish parties in its day. The first home built on Lafayette Square—then called President's Park—across from the White House, Decatur House was built for 19C naval hero Stephen Decatur. Today eight first-floor rooms, decorated to reflect the period when the Decaturs lived here, show off the museum's collection of 19C silver, textiles, ceramics, furniture and paintings.

Decatur's acts of heroism against the British in the War of 1812 earned him the rank of Captain and a substantial monetary prize. (In those days, the US Navy awarded cash prizes to men who captured enemy vessels.) With his newfound wealth, he commissioned eminent architect Benjamin H. Latrobe to design a home "fit for entertaining." The three-story structure cost Decatur $11,000. He and his wife, Susan, threw big parties here for DC politicos, but only for a brief 14 months. At the age of 41, the young commodore was killed in a duel with a discredited naval officer who held Decatur responsible for his disgrace. Bereft, Mrs. Decatur moved to a Georgetown town house and rented the Lafayette Square house to a succession of dignitaries.

---

**A Houseful of Statesmen and Socialites**

- Secretary of State Henry Clay lived here in the 1820s, calling it "the best private dwelling in the City."

- After Clay, Martin Van Buren, then secretary of State and soon to be president, occupied the house.

- In 1836 hotelier John Gadsby purchased the residence from Mrs. Decatur.

- Edward Fitzgerald Beale, a renowned Western adventurer, became owner of the house after the Civil War. For two decades Beale and his wife, Mary, were prominent members of the capital's social circles.

---

# Folger Shakespeare Library★

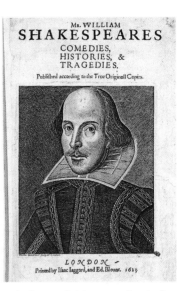

**[M]** *refers to map on inside front cover.*
*201 E. Capitol St. SE, between 2nd & 3rd Sts.*
*202-544-7077. www.folger.edu. Open year-round Mon–Sat 10am–4pm. Closed Sun & major holidays.*

Much ado about nothing? Quite the contrary. The Folger Library contains the world's largest collection of Shakespeare's printed works as well as rare Renaissance books and manuscripts. **Henry Clay Folger** (1857–1930) first became interested in Shakespeare while he was at Amherst College, where he went to hear a lecture on Shakespeare by Ralph Waldo Emerson. In 1889 Folger purchased his first rare book of Shakespeare's plays at auction, for a little over $100. He was hooked. The future chairman of the board of New York's Standard Oil Company and his wife, Emily, devoted themselves to gathering books, manuscripts, paintings and other objects relating to the Bard.

In the early 1900s, the Folgers decided that their collection needed a permanent home where the public could access it. Although they considered both Stratford-On-Avon (Shakespeare's hometown in England) and New York City as locations for their library, they finally settled on the nation's capital. Shortly after the cornerstone for the new Art Deco building was laid in 1930, Folger died unexpectedly following minor surgery. His library, which opened in 1932, is now administered by the trustees of Amherst College in Massachusetts.

**Great Hall** – In this 190ft-long room with its barrel-vaulted ceiling, the Library mounts two to three major exhibitions a year, selected from its collection of 310,000 books and manuscripts, 250,000 playbills, and 27,000 paintings, drawings, engravings and prints.

**Folger Theatre** – Designed to resemble the courtyard of an English Renaissance inn, this Elizabethan stage makes a perfect setting for Folger Theatre productions and early-music concerts. The Folger presents a full program of performances from Shakespeare's plays to poetry readings *(see Performing Arts)*.

### The Bard's Birthday Party

On April 27 each year the Folger celebrates Shakespeare's birthday with a program of Renaissance music and dance, and spontaneous performances of the Bard's work. This is the one day of the year when the Folger's Reading Rooms are open to the public. The kids can have their fortune told, write with quill pens, and participate in other Elizabethan crafts and games. Come join the fun and have a piece of cake for the Bard. As he would say, "All's well that ends well."

# Ford's Theatre and Petersen House ★

*10th St. NW, between E & F Sts. 202-426-6924. www.nps.gov/foth. Open year-round daily 9am–5pm. Closed Dec 25 & during rehearsals & performances.*

Going to see a play isn't normally a dangerous form of entertainment. But Abraham Lincoln's night out at Ford's Theatre in 1865 turned out to be the last thing he ever did. On the evening of April 14, 1865, just five days after General Robert E. Lee had surrendered to Union commander Ulysses S. Grant at Appomattox, Virginia, President and Mrs. Lincoln attended a performance of *Our American Cousin* at Ford's Theatre. The Lincolns were engrossed in the third act when John Wilkes Booth silently entered the box and shot the president at close range. Booth leaped over the balustrade and escaped on a horse that he had hidden in the theater alley.

The wounded president was carried across the street to a boarding house owned by a tailor named Petersen. As the night passed, Cabinet ministers, physicians and others gathered in the back parlor, while friends consoled Mrs. Lincoln in the front parlor. Lincoln never regained consciousness; he died there at 7:22am the following morning.

## Ford's Theatre

When John Ford opened the doors of this brick structure in 1863, it was one of the grandest theaters in the country, with a seating capacity of 2,500. After Lincoln's assassination, the federal government closed the theater. John Ford's announced intention to continue dramatic productions in the theater met with threats, so the War Department leased the building and began converting it into office space. In the mid-1960s Congress authorized a restoration of the playhouse to its 1865 appearance. Ford's Theatre reopened eight years later as both a memorial to Lincoln and an active playhouse *(see Performing Arts)*.

The box where Lincoln sat is decorated as it was on the night of April 14, 1865, with the settee that had been specially placed there for the president. In the basement, the refurbished **Lincoln Museum** *(same hours as the theater)* displays such artifacts as Booth's gun and the clothes Lincoln was wearing when he was shot.

### Petersen House

*516 10th St., across the street from the theater. Same hours as Ford's Theatre.*

The simple three-story brick row house where Lincoln died on April 15, 1865 was built in 1850 by tailor William Petersen. You can visit its three first-floor rooms, which are decorated with Victorian period furnishings.

# Frederick Douglass National Historic Site★

*1411 W St. SE. 202-426-5961. www.nps.gov/frdo. Open mid-Apr–mid-Oct daily 9am–5pm. Rest of the year daily 9am–4pm. Closed Jan 1, Thanksgiving Day, Dec 25. $2.*

Known as Cedar Hill, this white Victorian house was the last residence of black statesman, orator and abolitionist Frederick Douglass. The estate, which tops a shady knoll overlooking the Anacostia River, was originally built as a speculative property in the late 1850s by developer John Van Hook. When Douglass purchased the nine-acre estate from Van Hook, the house had never been lived in. Douglass expanded the property to 15 acres and added seven rooms to the rear of the house. In 1962 the house was donated to the National Park Service, who restored the estate and opened it to the public as a historic site.

Cedar Hill is decorated with Victorian furnishings and memorabilia, most of which belonged to the Douglass family. The ground floor consists of a formal parlor and a family parlor, a dining room, kitchen, Douglass' study and a pantry and washroom. The five bedrooms on the second floor include those of Douglass and his two successive wives. Behind the house, a small reconstructed stone building served as a second study, which Douglass called "the Growlery."

## Champion For Civil Rights

Born into slavery in Talbot County, Maryland about 1818, **Frederick Douglass**, christened Frederick Augustus Washington Bailey, was the son of a black mother and an unidentified white father. As a boy he worked as a house servant in Baltimore, where he was taught reading and writing by the household's white mistress. However, as a young man he was sent to work in the fields and suffered abuse at the hands of a notorious slave overseer.

In 1838 Douglass escaped bondage and fled north, settling with his wife Anna Murray in New Bedford, Massachusetts. In 1841 he became involved with the Massachusetts Anti-Slavery Society and soon became a respected abolitionist and publicist. Soon after the publication of his first book, *Narrative of the Life of Frederick Douglass, An American Slave* (1845), Douglass left for Europe. English sympathizers purchased Douglass' freedom in 1846 while he was abroad. During the Civil War Douglass helped recruit black troops; after the war he moved to Washington. During his years in Anacostia, Douglass received several presidential appointments to serve in district government. In 1895, after attending a women's rights meeting, Douglass died suddenly of a heart attack at his home.

## The Octagon★

*1799 New York Ave., NW.*
*202-638-3105.*
*www.archfoundation.org.*
*Open year-round Tue–Sun 10am–*
*4pm. Closed Mon, Jan 1, Thanksgiving*
*Day, Dec 25. $5.*

What kind of house can you build on a triangular lot? If you're Dr. William Thornton, the first architect of the US Capitol, you build a six-sided one with three stories. Now owned by the American Architectural Foundation, The Octagon ranks as the oldest museum in the US dedicated to architecture and design, and one of America's best examples of Federal-period architecture.

### What's In A Name?

If you're wondering why a house with only six sides is named after an eight-sided figure, you're not alone. No one, it seems, knows for sure how the house got its name. Architects and historians think that perhaps it was named for its round entrance hall. In the 18C, round rooms were often constructed with eight straight walls connected at angles. Builders would plaster over the angles of these so-called "octagon salons" so they'd appear smooth.

In the 1790s George Washington, anxious to develop the new federal city, convinced his friend Colonel John Tayloe to build a house several blocks west of present-day Lafayette Square.

A wealthy Virginia planter, Tayloe commissioned Dr. William Thornton to design a building for the triangular plot, formed by the intersection of New York Avenue and 18th Street. The Tayloes used the elegant house as their winter residence from its completion in 1801 until 1817, when they moved in permanently. President James Madison and his wife, Dolley, lived here for six months after the White House was burned by the British in 1814.

In 1902 the American Institute of Architects (AIA) purchased this architectural gem from the Tayloe family and began a meticulous restoration. Most recently restored between 1990 and 1995, the free-flowing interior of The Octagon, with its circular entrance hall and graceful oval staircase, now reflects the period when the Tayloes lived here.

**Treaty of Ghent Room** – At the round mahogany table in the center of this circular second-floor parlor, President Madison signed the Treaty of Ghent, which ended the War of 1812 with Great Britain. Signed by the British in Ghent, Belgium, on December 24, 1814, the document was brought to Washington three months later for Madison to sign.

## Tudor Place★

*1644 31st St. NW, two blocks east of Wisconsin Ave. between Q & R Sts. 202-965-0400. www.tudorplace.org. Visit by guided tour only, Tue–Fri 10am, 11:30am, 1pm & 2:30pm; Sat 10am–3pm hourly; Sun noon–3pm hourly. Closed major holidays. $6.*

Here you'll meet the Peter family—six generations of them—who lived in this Georgetown mansion for nearly 180 years. Tudor Place was completed in 1816 as the home of Thomas Peter and his wife, Martha Custis Peter, the granddaughter of Martha Washington.

In 1805, with the $8,000 inheritance Martha Peter received from her stepgrandfather, George Washington, the couple purchased an eight-acre city block in Georgetown Heights with sweeping views of the growing capital city and the Potomac River. Dr. William Thornton, a family friend and the first architect of the Capitol, was commissioned to design a stately home that would reflect the Peters' social status. The house, with its distinctive domed portico, took 11 years to build.

At her death in 1854, Martha Peter left the estate to the youngest of the three Peter daughters, Britannia Wellington Peter Kennon, who had been widowed after only a year of marriage. During the Civil War years, Britannia, a staunch Southern sympathizer (and relative of Robert E. Lee), allowed Union officers to use Tudor Place as a boardinghouse, stipulating only that "affairs of war not be discussed" in her presence.

The estate remained in the family until 1983, when it passed to the Tudor Place Foundation. Tudor Place opened to the public in 1988. Today the mansion displays some of the 8,000 household objects that the family owned over the years.

**Collections** – Highlights include George Washington's Sèvres porcelain dishes and Martha Washington's Chippendale tea table from Mount Vernon, as well as a fine collection of 19C European and American silver.

**Gardens** – The 5½ acres of grounds surrounding the house remain just as different generations of the Peter family planted them. Here you'll discover a boxwood ellipse, a geometric "knot" of flowers, and the China rose, "Old Blush," that Martha Peter herself planted along the south side of the house.

**N**eighborhoods give a city its character, and DC is no exception. From tony Georgetown to collegiate Foggy Bottom, and from the revitalized Penn Quarter to multiethnic Adams Morgan, Washington's neighborhoods all have a unique identity. Here are a few of our favorites.

## Georgetown★★

*Bounded on the south by the Potomac and on the east by Rock Creek. www.georgetowndc.com.*

When Washingtonians think of Georgetown, they usually think of nightlife. It's true that DC's choicest neighborhood contains more than its share of bars and clubs, but beyond the club scene there are wonderful restaurants and upscale shopping galore, not to mention a wealth of historic sights, museums and lovely Federal architecture lining quiet residential streets.

Georgetown began in the early 1700s as the site of a tobacco plantation. Positioned at the head of the Potomac River, the town thrived as a port and as the eastern terminus of the Chesapeake & Ohio Canal *(see sidebar, opposite)* into the late 18C. It was also during that time (1789) that the first Catholic institution of higher learning in the country, Georgetown College—now **Georgetown University**—was founded at the western edge of town.

Unfortunately, the efficiency of train travel gradually brought an end to barge transport. At the same time, the advent of steam navigation, which required deeper ports than the town could provide, put an end to Georgetown's shipping business. In 1871 the ailing town was consolidated with the District of Columbia.

Today Georgetown's residential streets, with their carefully restored Federal-style and mid-19C houses, ooze refinement. You never know who you might see here; many of the city's politicos and foreign dignitaries call this neighborhood home.

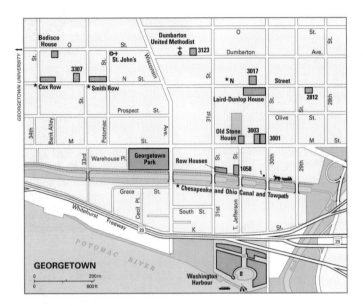

**GEORGETOWN**

0 — 200m
0 — 600ft

## What's What In Georgetown

**Heart of Georgetown** – It all happens along Wisconsin Avenue and M Street, which are lined with myriad restaurants, bars and trendy boutiques.

**Washington Harbour** – This riverfront complex of condos, offices, shops and restaurants incorporates a boardwalk and a terraced fountain court.

**Dumbarton Oaks** ★★ – *1703 32nd St. NW. See Historic Sites.*

**Tudor Place** ★ – *1644 31st St. NW. See Historic Sites.*

**Kreeger Museum** ★ – *2401 Foxhall Rd., NW. See Museums.*

**Rock Creek National Park** ★ – *Nature Center located at 5200 Glover Rd. NW. See Parks and Gardens.*

---

### Chesapeake & O Canal National Historical Park

*Georgetown visitor center is located at 1057 Thomas Jefferson St. NW, off M St. between 30th & 31st Sts. 202-653-5190. www.nps.gov/choh. Park open daily year-round dawn–dusk.*

Part of George Washington's dream to make the Potomac River navigable to western trade, the C&O Canal was intended to span 360mi from DC to the Ohio River. Although construction began on July 4, 1828, it would be more than 20 years before the "Great Canal Project" would be even partially realized.

The project was plagued by constant problems: expensive building materials, lack of skilled labor, and lengthy court battles with the competing Baltimore & Ohio Railroad to obtain titles for the right-of-way. Despite these setbacks, the first section of the canal, from Georgetown to Seneca, Maryland, opened in 1831. It wasn't until 1850 that the C&O Canal finally reached Cumberland, Maryland, a point that the B&O Railroad had arrived at eight years earlier. Beaten, the C&O Canal Company gave up. They had spent $22 million to build 184.5mi of canal.

In the 1950s, a proposal to pave over the "grand old ditch" was waylaid by conservationists, and in 1971 President Richard Nixon created the Cheasapeake & O National Historical Park. Today the C&O is the only remaining towpath canal in the US.

# Dupont Circle ★

*At the junction of Massachusetts, Connecticut & New Hampshire Aves., and 19th & P Sts. NW.*

Favored by business lunchers, chess players and the stroller set, this small but vibrant urban park is one of the capital's best people-watching spots. The bustling intersection forms the hub of a chic cosmopolitan neighborhood, which claims many of the city's finest boutiques, galleries and restaurants.

Dupont Circle's name honors Civil War hero Rear Admiral Samuel F. du Pont (1803–1865). A bronze statue of du Pont stood in the center of the circle until 1921, when the hero's family moved the memorial to Wilmington, Delaware. Shortly thereafter, the du Ponts replaced the statue with the marble fountain that now graces the circle. It was designed in 1921 by Daniel Chester French.

**The Phillips Collection** ★★ – *1600 21st St. NW. See Museums.*

**Society of the Cincinnati/Anderson House Museum** ★ – *2118 Massachusetts Ave. NW. 202-785-2040. Open year-round Tue–Sat 1pm–4pm. Closed major holidays. www.thesocietyofthecincinnati.addr.com.* The headquarters of this patriotic society, founded in 1783 by former Revolutionary War officers, displays war artifacts and an array of fine art collected by its previous owners, Larz and Isabel Anderson.

---

### Noshing On Connecticut Avenue

A longtime favorite of hungry literature lovers, **Kramerbooks & Afterwords** *(1517 Connecticut Ave. NW; 202-387-3825; www.kramers.com)* caters to Washington workaholics with hours from 7am to late-night daily (they're open all night Fri & Sat). Kramerbooks features a full-service bar and live entertainment along with its extensive menu of lunch and dinner fare.

**Marvelous Market** *(1511 Connecticut Ave. NW; 202-332-3690; www.marvelousmarket.com)* is a great place to put together your own carryout meal of homemade soup, pâtés, cheeses, and the market's own superb handmade artisan breads.

## Embassy Row

*Massachusetts Ave., between Scott Circle & Observatory Circle. Consulates are open for official business only. For a complete list of embassies in Washington, DC, check online at www.embassy.org.*

Embassy Row is the popular name of the two-mile portion of Massachusetts Avenue between Scott Circle and Observatory Circle where you'll find the greatest concentration of DC's 150 embassies. You'll recognize the chanceries (the embassies proper) and the ambassadors' residences (which may be separate from the chanceries) by the colorful flags or plaques that decorate their facades. The 2mi stretch of Massachusetts Avenue from 22nd Street to Observatory Circle is considered the most distinctive and elegant segment of Embassy Row. It developed with palatial homes in the first decade of the 20C. After the 1929 stock-market crash, the area's residents were forced to move to more modest quarters and foreign governments began buying up the mansions.

### Textile Museum★

*2320 S St. NW. 202-667-0441. www.textilemuseum.org. Open year-round Mon–Sat 10am–5pm, Sun 1pm–5pm. Closed Dec 24 & major holidays.*

If you're into handmade Oriental rugs, check out the Textile Museum while you're in the Embassy Row neighborhood. Started by George Hewitt Myers in 1925, this small private museum boasts a collection of 17,000 rugs and textiles, dating back to 3,000 BC.

## Foggy Bottom★

*Between Lafayette Square and Georgetown, south of Dupont Circle.*

Now home to George Washington University, the **John F. Kennedy Center for the Performing Arts**★★ *(see Performing Arts)* and the infamous Watergate condominium complex, this area west of the White House was once fog-shrouded bottomland. Breweries, glass plants and the city gas works sprang up here in the early 19C, when the area was home to a mix of Irish, Germans and African Americans. Waterfront warehouses, wharves and rows of narrow brick tenements added to the district's industrial character.

In 1912 **George Washington University** moved to the northern end of Foggy Bottom, bringing a collegiate air to the streets southeast of Washington Circle. After World War II, Foggy Bottom developed as an administrative quarter. Among the organizations located here today are the Department of Interior, the World Bank and the National Academy of Sciences.

Visiting all those museums, memorials and historic sights can get exhausting. Why not take a break and drink in the flowery sights and recreational activities in DC's most inviting parks and tranquil gardens?

## National Arboretum★

*3501 New York Ave. NE. Other entrance at 24th & R Sts. NE. 202-245-2726. www.usna.usda.gov. Grounds open year-round daily 8am–5pm. Closed Dec 25.*

If you happen to be visiting DC in late spring, make the National Arboretum a must-see. Here you'll find thousands of **azaleas**, setting the garden's hillsides ablaze with color. One of the largest arboretums in the country, this federally owned 446-acre tract situated on the gentle slopes of Mount Hamilton is a welcoming oasis in the midst of the warehouses of surrounding northeast Washington.

Established by Congress in 1927, the arboretum did not become a reality until 1947, when the first azaleas were planted. Washingtonians couldn't resist the spring display of these blooming shrubs. Local enthusiasm to see the azaleas spurred the gardens to open to the public in 1954. Today the arboretum's hills and valleys are covered in evergreens, wildflowers, azaleas, rhododendrons and dogwoods, whose spectacular blossoms seasonally attract hordes of visitors.

### Touring Tips

The arboretum is designed to be toured by car. Nine miles of paved roads lead past the various gardens and plant collections; parking areas are designated along the route. Another option is the 40-minute open-air tram tour, which gives you a history of the gardens as well as a look at the highlights (*mid-Apr–mid-Oct weekends only, 11:30am, 1pm, 2pm & 3pm*).

### Garden Delights

**National Bonsai and Penjing Museum★** – *Open daily 10am–3:30pm.* The walled Japanese garden complex, behind the modern administration building, includes the Penjing Museum, renowned for its outstanding collection of Japanese, Chinese and American bonsai.

**Herb Garden** – This two-acre garden features a formal 16C English knot garden; a rose garden with more than 80 varieties of antique roses; and 10 specialty gardens, where herbs are grouped according to their uses throughout history.

**National Capitol Columns** – Set atop a bluff, these columns originally flanked the east entrance of the Capitol building prior to its expansion in the late 1950s.

# Rock Creek National Park★

*Nature Center located at 5200 Glover Rd. NW. 202-895-6070. www.nps.gov/rocr. Park open year-round daily dawn–dusk. Nature Center open Wed–Sun 9am–5pm; closed major holidays.*

The capital's largest recreational area, Rock Creek Park covers some 2,100 acres astride scenic Rock Creek in northwest DC. You can easily while away a day here, indulging in as many—or as few—activities as you like. Start at the **Nature Center**, where you can get maps and information about what's going on in the park. This is also where many of the ranger-led programs start. A network of paved roads, hiking trails, and bicycle and bridle paths crisscross the vast park. And if that's not enough for you, there are 30 picnic areas, 25 tennis courts, and fields for soccer, football and field hockey. At the outdoor **Carter Barron Amphitheater** *(16th St. & Colorado Ave. NW; 202-426-0486)* you can catch concerts, dance, theater and music performances in summer.

## Historic Sights In The Park

**Old Stone House** – *3051 M. St. NW. Open Wed–Sun*. This 1765 stone house in Georgetown exemplifies the life lived by DC's ordinary citizens in Colonial days.

**Pierce Mill** – *Off Tilden St. NW, just west of Beach Dr*. Built in the 1820s, the mill operated on and off until 1993. Currently Pierce Mill is closed while crews repair its deteriorated wooden waterwheel and mechanical components.

**Battleground National Cemetery** – *6625 Georgia Ave*. This Civil War burial ground was established in July 1864, following the Battle of Fort Stevens.

---

### Horsing Around

With its 13mi of bridle paths, the park makes a great place to ride. Located next to the Nature Center, the Rock Creek Park Horse Center offers riding lessons, guided trail rides and pony rides for the wee ones. There's even an equitation field in the park. For information, call the Horse Center *(202-362-0118; www.rockcreekhorsecenter.com)*.

---

# US Botanic Garden

*On the Mall along 1st St., between Maryland Ave. & C St. 202-225-8333. www.usbg.gov. Conservatory open year-round daily 10am–5pm.*

A plant conservatory across from the Capitol? Sure, there's been a botanic garden there since 1850, when the collection of exotic specimens brought from the South Seas by a team of US explorers was housed on the Mall. The present conservatory, begun in 1931, has just completed a four-year renovation. Now decked out with a new state-of-the-art automated environmental-control system, the nation's living-plant museum showcases some 4,000 specimens, including seasonal floral exhibits, towering subtropical plants and flowering orchids.

Situated across Independence Avenue, the formal plantings at **Bartholdi Park** provide a colorful setting for the cast-iron **Bartholdi Fountain**, sculpted by Frédéric-Auguste Bartholdi, creator of the Statue of Liberty. Work has also begun on a new **National Garden**, which will include a three-acre public garden and an environmental learning center, to open in 2005.

In a city that boasts the country's largest concentration of PhDs, you have to wonder what they do for fun here. Never fear, DC has more than its share of outdoor activities and quirky tours to amuse you once you get bored with all the serious stuff.

## C&O Canal Barge Ride

*Rides ($8) depart May–mid-Nov Wed–Sun from the C&O Canal National Historical Park visitor center in Georgetown. 1057 Thomas Jefferson St. NW. For schedules, call 202-653-5190. www.nps.gov/choh.*

Travel back in time on a mule-drawn canal boat. Guides in mid-19C period costume will tell you the story of the canal and what life was like in Georgetown's early days. During the hour-long trip down the Georgetown section of the C&O, you'll get to go through one of the canal's original lock lifts.

## Hike or Bike the C&O Towpath ★ to Old Angler's Inn

*Pick up the towpath in Georgetown, ½ block south of M St. between 29th & 35th Sts. NW. For information, stop at the C&O Canal National Historical Park visitor center (1057 Thomas Jefferson St. NW; off M St. between 30th & 31st Sts.). 202-653-5190. www.nps.gov/choh.*

A quiet walk or bike ride along the old **C&O Canal towpath** will give you exercise with a view—of both lovely scenery and the area's historic past *(see Neighborhoods/ Georgetown).* From Georgetown, follow the towpath about 12mi north. Between mile marker 12 and 13, you'll find the **Old Angler's Inn**, a wonderful place to rest and have lunch or a drink on the outdoor terrace. The rustic inn, which has been serving travelers along the canal route since 1860, now features excellent New American cuisine *(10801 MacArthur Blvd., Potomac, MD; 301-299-9097; www.oldanglersinn.com; open for lunch & dinner Tue–Sun).*

## National Sculpture Garden – Fun For All Seasons

*On the Mall at 7th St. & Constitution Ave. NW. 202-737-4215. www.nga.gov.*

In summer and winter, you'll find fun afoot at the National Gallery of Art's Sculpture Garden. Every Friday night *(5pm–8pm, rain or shine)* in summer, there are free **jazz concerts** in front of the Pavilion Café, which stays open during performances.

A favorite with Washingtonians, **ice-skating** on the Sculpture Garden's rink is a great way to spend a chilly winter afternoon or evening *(on the Mall at Madison Dr. & 9th St. NW; open mid-Nov–mid-Mar, weather permitting; Mon–Thu*

*10am–11pm, Fri & Sat 10am–midnight, Sun 11am–9pm; $6/2hr session; skate rental $2.50, photo ID required).* If you're in the city at Christmastime, be sure to walk over to the Ellipse *(Constitution Ave. between 15th & 17th Sts. NW)* after your skating session to see the National Christmas tree.

## Paddle the Potomac River

*Rentals available at Thompson Boat Center, 2900 Virginia Ave., at the corner of Rock Creek Pkwy. in Georgetown. 202-333-9543. www.thompsonboatcenter.com. Rentals available mid-Mar–Oct daily 8am–6pm. Rentals start at $8hr.*

If you're hankering to get out on the water, you can rent canoes and kayaks by the hour or by the day at **Thompson Boat Center**. From Thompson's it's an easy paddle to Roosevelt Island *(see below)* or the Georgetown waterfront. Landlubbers can rent bikes here, too *(mid-Mar–Sept)* for a ride along the C&O Canal towpath or the Rock Creek Park bike path *(see Parks and Gardens)*.

## Scandal Tour

*Departs from Old Post Office Pavilion, 1100 Pennsylvania Ave. NW. Apr–Labor Day, Sat 1pm. Reservations required. 202-783-7212. www.gnpcomedy.com. $30.*

What skeletons lurk in the White House closets? What Congressman took a moonlight skinny-dip in the Tidal Basin with stripper Fannie Fox? You'll find out the answers to these probing questions and more on the hilarious two-hour Scandal Tour, led by members of DC's Gross National Product comedy troupe. (Leave the kids at home for this one.)

## Spydrive

*Held one Sat/month at 9:30am. Your ticket will instruct you where to meet your tour leader. Reservations required. 202-432-7328 or 866-779-3748. www.spytrek.com. $55.*

You'll never look at Washington, DC the same way again after you take this 2½-hour undercover tour. Led by former intelligence officers from the FBI, CIA and Russia's KGB, Spydrive takes you on a bus past sites where real spies lived, worked and operated. You'll see dead drops, signal sites and meeting places—and you thought the capital's monuments were just historic sites!

## Theodore Roosevelt Island

*Access only from the northbound lane of George Washington Memorial Pkwy. From DC, take GW Pkwy. north past the exit for Key Bridge; the island will be on your right. Park and walk across the footbridge. No bicycles permitted. 703-289-2500. www.nps.gov/this.*

A striking statue of President Theodore Roosevelt greets you as you enter this 91-acre woodland preserve, which makes a fitting memorial to the naturalist for whom it's named. Located near Arlington, Virginia, the forested island on the Potomac River is threaded by 2½mi of nature trails. Take a peaceful walk through the woodlands and marshes, where you'll see a variety of wildlife, especially birds. You can fish here, too, but permits are required for anyone over 16.

**W**hile Washington, DC conjures up images of political debates and daily crises on the House floor, government officials aren't the only ones making scenes around the nation's capital. Don't let the city's straight-laced atmosphere fool you—from symphonies to pop stars, DC knows how to put on a show. Round up your chorus line and head out to these top performance spots.

## John F. Kennedy Center ★★

*New Hampshire Ave. at Rock Creek Pkwy. NW. Guided tours available. Information: 202-416-8340. Tickets: 202-467-4600. www.kennedy-center.org.*

A gleaming horizontal mass, ranking as one of the country's leading cultural institutions, this "living memorial" to the 35th US president is home to the **National Symphony Orchestra**. A wide spectrum of world-class entertainment—from tenor Placido Domingo to comedian Bill Cosby—is offered in its six theaters. When you enter the 630ft-long **Grand Foyer**, with its prominent bronze **bust** of President Kennedy, you'll be awed by the 60-ft high mirrors from Belgium and the eighteen crystal chandeliers from Sweden.

## Ford's Theatre ★

*10th St., between E & F Sts. NW. Guided tours available: 202-426-6924. Tickets: 202-347-4833. For description, see Historic Sites.*

John Wilkes Booth's assassination of President Abraham Lincoln in 1865 quickly put Ford's Theatre on the map. Afterwards, as national chaos ensued, a curtain fell on theatrical productions for nearly a hundred years, until a restoration effort began in the 1960s. Today, Ford's Theatre thrives again as a living tribute to Lincoln's passion for the performing arts. American life takes center stage in productions ranging from musicals to star-studded TV specials.

## Arena Stage

*1101 Sixth St. SW. 202-488-4377. www.arena-stage.org.*

As the first nonprofit theater in the US (c.1950), Arena Stage has been synonymous with artistic expression and diversity. Arena presents both classic and contemporary theatrical pieces; recent offerings have included Molière's *Misanthrope* and *Mrs. Bob Cratchit's Wild Christmas Binge*. The 120-seat **Old Vat Room**, a converted brewery downstairs, hosts works in development.

## Folger Theatre

*201 E. Capitol St. SE. Guided tours available: 202-544-4600. Tickets: 202-544-7077. www.folger.edu.*

Education and entertainment are powerful partners at the Folger Shakespeare Theatre, the performing-arts extension to the library of the same name *(see Historic Sites.).* Performances here promote the social value and beauty of Shakespeare's works. With presentations like *All's Well that Ends Well* and *The Comedy of Errors*, plus corresponding lectures, this showcase of Elizabethan culture attracts scholars and theater-lovers alike.

## National Theatre

*1321 Pennsylvania Ave. NW. 202-628-6161.*
*Tickets: 800-447-7400.*
*www.nationaltheatre.org.*

What do Warren Beatty and Shirley MacLaine have in common? Besides being brother and sister, they both worked at the National (Warren as a doorman, Shirley as an usher) before becoming stars in their own right. Just three blocks from the White House, the "Theatre of Presidents" stages stellar traveling Broadway shows like *Cats!* and *The Wizard of Oz.*

### Low On Cash?

Get discounted day-of-show tickets at **TICKETplace** at the Old Post Office Pavilion *(1100 Pennsylvania Ave. NW; open Tues–Fri noon–6pm, Sat 11am–5pm; 202-842-5387; www.cultural-alliance.org/tickets).* They offer half-price ticket sales for most performances in Washington, DC when available. Check the Web site for a listing of current and advance sales.

## Warner Theatre

*13th & E Sts. NW. 202-783-4000. www.warnertheatre.com.*

The Warner began in the vaudeville days of the Roaring Twenties. By 1945, the theatre had adopted a movies-only policy, and offered everything from classics like *Ben Hur* to pornographic films in the 1970s. After extensive renovations, Warner Theatre re-emerged in 1992. It continues to draw top recording artists and a full array of dance and theatrical productions.

### Capitol Steps

*Fri & Sat nights at the Ronald Reagan Building & International Trade Center, 1300 Pennsylvania Ave. NW. 202-312-1555. www.capsteps.com.*

Just in case you thought Capitol Hill was all about political correctness, this two-hour comedy show will have you rolling in the aisles. Billed as "musical political satire" and performed by current and former congressional staffers, the Capitol Steps evolved from an office Christmas party skit in 1981. These popular political satirists have kept audiences (including several presidents) roaring with their irreverent spoofs of Washington politics. Musical parodies such as "We Arm the World," "Between Iraq and a Hard Place," and "Fools on the Hill" make for unforgettable fun.

## Wolf Trap Farm Park

*1645 Trap Rd., off Rte. 7 in Vienna, VA. 703-255-1900. Tickets: 703-255-1860. www.wolf-trap.org.*

Grab a picnic dinner and a blanket and settle back under the stars. From Beethoven to the Beach Boys, the Wolf Trap Foundation in nearby northern Virginia presents a kaleidoscope of performances, including dance, theater and its own opera company. The **Filene Center** outdoor amphitheater seats 7,000, while **The Barns** accommodate 352 people for more intimate stagings.

## Woolly Mammoth

*917 M St. NW. 202-289-2443. Tickets: 202-393-3939. www.woollymammoth.net.*

American values may be upheld by Congress, but they are held up for scrutiny by performers at the Woolly Mammoth, DC's edgy theater company, established in 1978 by two young New York actors. *Goodnight Desdemona* and *The Rocky Horror Show* have both graced the stage here, alongside up-and-coming plays from new writers.

**D**espite the policy-making and other serious doings that go on in this city, DC likes to kid around. In fact, many of its Very Important People are still young at heart. These picks are guaranteed to please "kids" of all ages. And best of all, many of them are free!

## National Air and Space Museum★★★

*On the Mall at Independence Ave. & 6th St. SW. 202-357-2700. www.nasm.si.edu. For hours, see Museums.*

The world's most-visited museum is a sure-fire hit with kids. From IMAX movies to lunar modules, it's all about flying. See the Wright Brothers *1903 Flyer* and Lindbergh's *Spirit of St. Louis*. Touch a moon rock. Imagine what it would be like to hurtle through earth's atmosphere in a cramped space capsule. Big kids will want to take a turn at **Flight Simulator Zone**.
In this simulator 12ft above the ground, you control the gut-wrenching barrel rolls, upside-down loops, and other aerobatic feats, enhanced by a 58-inch virtual-reality screen and high-tech sound effects.

## National Zoological Park★★

*3001 Connecticut Ave. NW. Other entrance on Beach Dr. 202-673-4717. www.natzoo.si.edu. Grounds open Apr–Oct daily 6am–8pm; buildings open 10am–6pm. Rest of the year grounds close at 6pm; buildings close at 4:30pm. Closed Dec 25.*

Plan at least a half-day to see this 163-acre urban zoo, set in the northern section of Rock Creek Park. Housing some 28,000 animals representing 435 different species, the zoo was created in 1887 as the Department of Living Animals, and was originally located on the Mall. In 1889 Congress appropriated funds for the creation of a true zoological park, to be administered by the Smithsonian Institution. A 163-acre tract above Rock Creek Park was purchased, and renowned landscape architect Frederick Law Olmsted laid out plans for the new zoo. Now revamped and modernized, the zoo continues its mission to "study, celebrate and protect animals and their habitats."

### DC's Darlings

In 1972, the zoo's first breeding pair of Giant Pandas, Hsing Hsing and Ling Ling, captured the hearts of Washingtonians, who came to see them by the thousands. No less popular are the newest pair, Tian Tian (b.1997) and Mei Xiang (b.1998), who arrived in the US from China in December 2000. The pandas quickly made themselves at home in their new habitat, which includes air- and water-cooled grottoes, sand wallows and climbing structures in its 17,500sq ft outdoor area. The People's Republic of China receives $1 million per year for the loan of the pandas; these funds will assist efforts to preserve the wild panda population.

## What's Hot At The Zoo?

**Panda House**★★ – This is the home of the zoo's most popular inhabitants, Giant Pandas Tian Tian and Mei Xiang.

**African Savanna**★ – The savanna re-creates the dry tropical east African grassland, where lions and cheetahs coexist with hippos, zebras and gazelles.

**Think Tank**★ – The zoo's oldest building (1906) now contains exhibits that detail animal thought processes and communication skills. Watch keepers teach symbolic language to resident orangutans, who commute between the Think Tank and the Great Ape House via vine-like cables suspended 20ft over the zoo's pathways.

**Reptile Discovery Center** – The 1929 Byzantine-style center houses the world's largest lizard, the Komodo dragon, along with other lizards and a host of snakes.

# ImaginAsia at the Sackler Gallery★★

*On the Mall at 1050 Independence Ave. SW. Programs are held in the classroom on the 2nd floor of the gallery. 202-357-2700. www.asia.si.edu. For hours, see Museums.*

Art doesn't have to be boring. At the Sackler and at its sister museum, the **Freer Gallery**★★ *(Jefferson Dr. at 12th St. SW; 202-357-4880)*, families can tour the exhibits with the help of a self-guided tour booklet, courtesy of the ImaginAsia program. After you've toured the exhibit, the kids (ages 6-14) can make their own art project based on what they saw. *Children must be accompanied by an adult*.

# National Museum of Natural History★★

*On the Mall at 10th St & Constitution Ave. NW. 202-357-2700. www.nmnh.si.edu. For hours, see Museums.*

Goldilocks may have thought the wolf's teeth were big, but they were nothing compared to the choppers on the museum's *Tyrannosaurus rex*. T-rex is joined by buddies "Hatcher" the triceratops and an 87ft-long *Diplodocus* in the first-floor **Dinosaurs** exhibit.

Scared of big things? The **Insect Zoo** *(2nd floor)* has lots of little things—it's just that some of them are pretty creepy. See an ant colony, touch a tarantula (if you dare!) and find out why your home and yard are favorite hangouts for insect critters. Check out the tarantula feedings *(Tue–Fri 10:30am, 11:30am & 1:30pm; weekends 11:30am, 12:30pm & 1:30pm)*.

## Hands-On Science Center at National Museum of American History ★★

*Constitution Ave., between 12th & 14th Sts. NW. 202-357-2700. www.american history.si.edu. Open Tue–Fri 12:30pm–5pm, weekends 10am–5pm (hours are subject to change; call to check before you visit).*

Kids (age 5-12) who like to get into everything will be in heaven here. Designed to complement the museum's Science in Everyday Life exhibit *(2nd floor)*, the Hands-On Science Center lets kids experiment with lasers, measure radioactive hot spots, make simple electrical circuits and separate food dyes used in soft drinks—and that's just for starters. *Children must be accompanied by an adult.*

## Carousel on the Mall

*On the Mall, in front of the Arts & Industries Building (between the Smithsonian Castle and the Hirshhorn Gallery). 202-357-2700. www.si.edu. Mar–early Sept 10am–5:30pm; rest of the year 11am–5pm. Closed Dec 25. $1.75.*

Who can't resist a carousel? A ride on the world's oldest carousel, which still goes 'round and 'round on the Mall, is a great way to give the kids—and maybe you, too—a break from museum-going.

## Discovery Theater at the Smithsonian

*In the Arts & Industries Building, 900 Jefferson Dr. SW. 202-357-1500. www.discoverytheater.org. Open Sept–July Mon–Fri 10am & 11:30am. No shows in Aug. $5 adults, $4 children.*

From African rhythms to magic shows, Discovery Theater entertains the younger set with puppets, storytellers, actors, dancers and mimes. This on-going series of live performances especially for kids features a dozen performances each season. With themes including international folk tales and American history, your child just may learn something, too.

## National Aquarium

*14th St. & Constitution Ave. NW. 202-482-2825. www.nationalaquarium.com. Open year-round daily 9am–5pm. Closed Dec 25. $3.50 adults, $1 children.*

This small aquarium, established in 1873, ranks as the nation's oldest. Tanks here swim with some 1,500 specimens of marine life. You'll see sharks, piranhas, sea turtles, moray eels, sea horses and toad-fish, among a host of other denizens of the deep. Don't miss the daily talks and feedings *(2pm)* by animal keepers at the aquarium. The topic is sharks on Monday, Wednesday and Saturday. Keepers chew the fat about piranhas on Tuesday, Thursday and Sunday. Get a grip on alligators every Friday.

## National Geographic Society Explorer's Hall

*17th & M Sts. NW. 202-857-7588. www.nationalgeographic.com/explorer. Open year-round Mon–Sat 9am–5pm, Sun 10am–5pm. Closed Dec 25.*

Kids love these interactive exhibits, done as only the Geographic can do them. In the recent past, visitors to Explorer's Hall have been able to meet Dinosaurs of the Sahara; explore the ends of the earth with Sir Edmund Hillary, Everest and Beyond; and visit a Robot Zoo. New experiences are waiting for you!

## Paddleboats on the Tidal Basin

*At the west end of the Mall, just south of the Washington Monument.*

No visit to DC is complete without a turn around the Tidal Basin in a paddle-boat on a sunny day. You can rent boats by the hour from the Tidal Basin Boat House *(15th St. & Maine Ave. SW; open daily 10am–6pm; $8/hr for 2-passenger boat; $16/hr for 4-passenger boat; 202-484-0206; photo ID required)*. This is great fun for the whole family.

## Puppet Co. Playhouse

*At Glen Echo Park, off MacArthur Blvd. in Glen Echo, MD. 301-320-6688. www.thepuppetco.org. Performances year-round Wed, Thu & Fri 10am & 11:30am, weekends 11:30am & 1pm. $6 (free for children under 2).*

What kid doesn't like puppet shows? Since 1989 the 200-seat playhouse in Glen Echo Park has been staging puppet productions for children. The 20-show repertory includes such classics as *The Velveteen Rabbit*, *Jungle Book* and *The Nutcracker*. A combination of hand puppets, body puppets, shadow puppets, rod puppets and marionettes are used in the productions, which change about every six weeks.

## Washington Doll's House and Toy Museum

*5236 44th St. NW. 202-244-0024. www.dollshousemuseum.com. Open Tue–Sat 10am–5pm, Sun noon–5pm. Closed Mon, Jan 1, Thanksgiving Day & Dec 25. $4 adults, $2 children.*

Kids didn't always have video games to amuse them. Why, in the old days, children played with dolls and dollhouses and wooden toys, like the rooms full of antique playthings that you'll find at this museum in upper northwest DC. Come see the revolving musical tree at Christmastime.

# Must Shop

**S**ave room in your suitcase: Washington, DC is a wonderful place to pick up a few things you really don't need. Trendy boutiques and galleries punctuate the city's neighborhoods, while immense suburban malls and outlet centers are just a short drive away.

### To Market, To Market

Don't miss spending a weekend morning at one of DC's neighborhood markets. At **Eastern Market** *(225 7th St. SE; www.easternmarket.net)* on capitol hill locals sift through fresh produce, baked goods, and succulent meats and cheeses. On Sundays, **Georgetown Flea Market** *(Wisconsin Ave., between S & T Sts. NW; www.georgetownflea market.com)* stocks an unbeatable selection of home furnishings, old records, and vintage clothing.

## Georgetown★★

*Wisconsin & M Sts. NW. www.georgetowndc.com.*

Washington, DC's best-known shopping district features upscale retailers like Betsey Johnson and Swedish retailer H&M along with standbys like Gap and Victoria's Secret. Unique specialty stores include accessory haven **Hats in the Belfry** *(1237 Wisconsin Ave. NW; 202-342-2006; www.hatsinthebelfry.com)*, and **Shake Your Booty** *(3225 M St. NW; 202-333-6524)*, which answers women's cries for affordable, comfortable and fashionable shoes. The four-level Victorian Mall, **Georgetown Park** *(3222 M St. NW; 202-298-5577)* features a mix of upscale stores and fine-art galleries.

## Union Station★

*50 Massachusetts Ave. NE. 202-289-1908. www.unionstationdc.com.*

You can pick up some last-minute souvenirs at Washington, DC's glorious Union Station. Designed by Daniel Burnham, the magnificent 1907 Beaux-Arts building was recently refurbished and now houses one of the District's most popular shopping and dining complexes. Known retailers such as Origins and Ann Taylor join specialty shops, a food court and fine restaurants here beneath the breathtaking barrel-vaulted ceiling.

## Museum Gift Shops

Psst, here's a Washingtonian shopping secret—museum gift shops. You can find some truly unique items in the shops at these and other DC museums:

**National Building Museum** *(401 F St.; 202-272-2448; www.nbm.org)* — Ergonomic office supplies.

**International Spy Museum** *(800 F St. NW; 202-393-7798; www.spymuseum.org)* — Spy gadgets and disguises.

**National Gallery of Art** *(Madison Dr., between 3rd & 7th Sts. NW; 202-737-4215; www.nga.gov)* — Museum-inspired jewelry, scarves, prints and notecards.

**Smithsonian Institution** *(on the Mall; 202-357-2700; www.si.edu)* – At the museums on the Mall, you can buy everything from Astronaut ice cream (Air & Space) and presidential campaign memorabilia (American History) to semi-precious gemstones and dinosaur assembly kits (Natural History). *For more information, see Museums.*

## U Street

*14th & U Sts. NW.*

Head to the newly revitalized U Street neighborhood for a crash course in home décor. Poking fun at the city's quest for statehood, **Home Rule** *(1807 14th St., NW; 202-797-5544)* is where you go to find a shower curtain that resembles bubble wrap, or a toilet plunger shaped like an Academy Award. Next door, **Go Mama Go!** *(1809 14th St. NW; 202-299-0850; www.gomamago.com)* packs goodies from an international bazaar into an urban storefront. Or let your shopping odyssey take you a block over and a few decades back in time to **Millennium Decorative Arts** *(1528 U St. NW; 202-462-4444)* for housewares, clothing, and knickknacks from the past century.

## Suburban Malls

Located in nearby Arlington, Virginia, **Fashion Centre at Pentagon City** features 160 other stores, and it's linked to DC via the Metrorail system *(4mi south of DC, 1100 S. Hayes St.; take I-395 South to Exit 8/Washington Blvd./Ridge Rd.; 703-415-2400; www.fashioncentrepentagon.com).*

**Tysons Corner Center** claims more than 250 stores, with anchors Nordstrom, Bloomingdales and Lord & Taylor *(off I-495 on Rte. 7; 1961 Chain Bridge Rd., McLean, VA; 703-847-7300; www.shoptysons.com).* Just across Chain Bridge Road, the three-level **Galleria at Tysons II** *(2001 International Dr.; 703-827-7700; www.tysonsgalleria.com)* offers upscale shopping in Neiman Marcus, Saks Fifth Avenue and more than 100 specialty stores.

### Bargain Hunting

Looking for a good deal? The DC metropolitan area is surrounded by outlet malls. The largest, **Potomac Mills** boasts more than 220 discount stores *(25mi south of DC in Prince William, VA; take I-95 South to Exit 158B/Prince William Pkwy.; 703-643-1855; www.millscorp.com).*

**Arundel Mills** is home to more than 200 retailers, as well as a 24-screen movieplex *(27mi north of DC in Hanover, MD; take I-295 North to Arundel Mills Blvd.; 410-540-5100; www.millscorp.com).*

# Must Be Seen: Nightlife

**A**lthough it's largely populated by stodgy politicians, pugnacious lobbyists, and more lawyers than you can shake a stick at, DC *does* like to let its hair down now and then. Whether its boogying or listening to blues music, Washingtonians love their nightlife. Here's where the cognoscenti head after all those boring receptions on the Hill.

## The Black Cat

*1831 14th St. NW, U St. area. 202-667-7960. www.blackcatdc.com.*

Music lovers flock to The Black Cat for a sneak preview of some of rock's rising stars. With ample space that can hold 550 fans, The Black Cat fills with pierced and tattooed punk- and alternative-music fiends. The familiar U Street haunt is co-owned by former Nirvana drummer and current Foo Fighter Dave Grohl.

### What's Up?

For the latest on who's playing where, consult the Friday Weekend section of the *Washington Post*, or check the entertainment pages online at www.washingtonpost.com.

## Blues Alley

*1073 Wisconsin Ave. NW, Georgetown. 202-337-4141. www.bluesalley.com.*

Few Washington clubs have enjoyed the success and notoriety of George-town's Blues Alley, which has been praised by no less than Dizzy Gillespie. Some of the biggest names in jazz have played and recorded albums in the venerable venue, tucked away in a Georgetown alley.

## Bohemian Caverns

*2001 11th St. NW, U St. area. 202-299-0800. www.bohemiancaverns.com.*

One of DC's best jazz spots in the days of Duke Ellington, Bohemian Caverns recently reopened with a fresh new look and a pleasing lineup of performers. An upscale restaurant occupies the upper level, while live music trickles up from the caverns below.

## Cities

*18th St. NW, Adams Morgan. 202-328-7194.*

Brimming with smartly dressed professionals, Cities is quite a departure from the casual bars that line the streets of Adams Morgan. If you're looking to sample the cuisine, the nightlife or the culture of far-off places, Cities is worth the visit—the club is themed after an international city, which changes every few months.

## Eighteenth Street Lounge

*1212 18th St. NW, Adams Morgan. 202-466-3922. www.eslmusic.com.*

Celebrity residents and visitors are often spotted in ESL (as it's known to locals), one of Dupont Circle's hippest nightlife spots. Bouncers guard the beautiful property—a historic mansion that was once home to Teddy Roosevelt—and maintain a strict admissions policy (no jeans or sneakers).

## Madam's Organ

*2461 18th St. NW, Adams Morgan. 202-667-5370. www.madamsorgan.com.*

"Sorry, we're open" reads the mural outside, just below a busty redhead's boldly painted portrait. The bright colors and brazen sarcasm of Madam's Organ have made it one of the most familiar sites in DC. Inside, it's just as quirky. Take the stairs up to Big Daddy's Love Lounge & Pick-Up Joint, but beware—it's aptly named.

## MCCXXIII

*1223 Connecticut Ave. NW, Dupont Circle. 202-822-1800. www.1223.com.*

Billing itself as Washington's "Premier Champagne and Caviar Club," this is a place for those who take nightlife seriously. MCCXXIII wards off the not-so-chic Dupont Circle denizens from its classy clientele.

## 9:30 Club

*815 V St. NW, at 9th St. & Vermont Ave., U St. area. 202-265-0930. www.930.com.*

This storied club can pack in 1,200 people to listen to an enticing lineup of local and national acts. The edgy 9:30 attracts a young crowd ("all ages, all the time") who don't mind that the club is standing-room only—there are no seats.

## Polly Esther's

*605 12th St. NW, Downtown. 202-737-1970. www.pollyesthers.com.*

If you're looking for a no-frills, no-pressure place to dance, you can't beat Polly Esther's. Three floors, dedicated to the 1970s, 80s and 90s, pulse with familiar music. Drinks, too, bear the names of pop-culture icons from each decade, and era-appropriate movie and television clips play on big-screen TVs.

### Hotel Hot Spots

Some of the hottest spots in town are housed in Washington's hip new hotels. Sex and attitude permeate the menu of adventurous drinks at **Bar Rouge** *(1315 16th St. NW; 202-232-8000; www.rouge-dc.com)* at the Hotel Rouge. Choose a sultry Femme Fatale or Sin on the Rocks. At the Hotel Helix, the retro **Helix Lounge** *(1430 Rhode Island Ave. NW; 202-462-9001; www.hotelhelix.com)* serves Pabst Blue Ribbon beer in a room drenched in white vinyl.

## Third Edition

*1218 Wisconsin Ave. NW, Georgetown. 202-333-3700. www.thethirdedition.com.*

This Georgetown mainstay served as the backdrop for the movie *St. Elmo's Fire* and has hosted many a college student since it opened in 1969. On Wednesday through Saturday nights, a dance party erupts on the upper level, leaving the mellow downstairs beer-sippers in the wake of rock classics. In the summertime, the lively Tiki Bar offers one of Georgetown's few opportunities for outdoor nightlife off the riverfront.

**E**ven Washington, DC's biggest egos need to be massaged once in a while. Tired tourists and power players alike can find refuge in a pedicure or facial at the many day spas in the nation's capital. From downtown to Georgetown, there's no shortage of spas that cater to the hard-working politicos, social activists and soccer moms of the Washington, DC metropolitan area.

## Andre Chreky

*1604 K St. NW. 202-293-9393.*
*www.andrechreky.com.*

One of Washington's most revered hair salons doubles as a day spa, where you can pop in for a quick manicure or melt into a relaxing massage. Located in the bustling business district, it's a popular stop for hardworking lawyers and lobbyists. Indulge in complimentary pastries and cappuccinos while you await your treatment.

## Bluemercury

*3059 M St. NW., 202-965-1300; 1745*
*Connecticut Ave. NW, 202-462-1300.*
*www.bluemercury.com.*

This Washington and New York-based purveyor of upscale beauty products gets rave reviews for its pain-free waxing and high-tech oxygen facials. With locations in Georgetown and Dupont Circle, the spa draws a young, fashion-conscious crowd for its stylish treatments and funky cosmetics.

## Capital City Club and Spa

*1001 16th St. NW. 202-639-4300. www.hilton.com.*

Housed in the Capital Hilton, the Capital City Club and Spa is a popular 11,000sq ft workout facility that offers an array of spa packages and treatment options. After an invigorating workout, treat yourself to a Reiki healing session or a deep-tissue massage. Instead of that 5pm martini, try the "Happy Hour Alternative," featuring an hour-long massage, a therapeutic facial, and a spa manicure and pedicure.

## Celadon

*1180 F St. NW. 202-347-3333. www.celadonspa.com.*

Hot-stone massages and anti-aging manicures beckon at this oasis, nestled among downtown office buildings. Celadon's treatment rooms are washed in muted shades of green and illuminated solely by aromatherapy candles. Sugar scrubs and alpha-hydroxy facials make city life a little more bearable.

## Elizabeth Arden Red Door

*5225 Wisconsin Ave. NW. 202-362-9890. www.reddoorsalons.com. Additional locations in Arlington, Reston, and Vienna, Virginia.*

Classic Red Door treatments are available at four locations throughout the metropolitan area. A favorite choice for Washington celebrities, local brides and famous faces, Elizabeth Arden helped ready Chelsea Clinton for her high school prom.

## Four Seasons Fitness Club and Spa

*Four Seasons Hotel, 2800 Pennsylvania Ave. NW. 202-944-2022. www.fourseasons.com.*

Frequently voted best in the city, this Georgetown landmark takes a cue from the Four Seasons spa in Bali for its luxurious skin treatments and massages. Your skin will never feel as smooth as after the spa's signature lanna herbal body polish or Bali coconilla scrub.

## Georgette Klinger Skin Care

*5345 Wisconsin Ave. NW. 202-686-8880. www.georgetteklinger.com.*

One of the most enduring names in skin care still delivers some of the finest facials in the metropolitan area. Klinger's facials are personalized to defend against stress, aging, acne, or other antagonists. The Georgetown spa also offers hair and scalp treatments, massage, nail care and microdermabrasion.

## The Grooming Lounge

*1745 L St. NW. 202-466-8900. www.groominglounge.com.*

Who said indulgence was just for women? While most of the city's spas welcome male patrons with "just for men" packages, this one takes it a step further. The Grooming Lounge is a downtown gentlemen's salon, where guys can enjoy a hot-lather shave or a business manicure. The lounge also offers assistance in tackling such embarrassing problems as back hair and unibrows.

## The Sports Club/LA Splash

*Ritz-Carlton Washington, 1170 22nd St. NW. 202-974-6601. www.sportsclubla.com.*

A favorite retreat for visitors and Washingtonians, showy Splash delights clients with its signature Soft Pack flotation device. Once you're unwrapped from this unique water-filled blanket, you'll find yourself blissfully limp and feeling virtually weightless. Splash is also known for some of the city's most relaxing massages and offers half-day, full-day and week-long packages.

Just across the river from DC, the sprawling suburbs of Northern Virginia lie within easy commuting distance of the city. That's where you'll find historic sites including George Washington's plantation and venerable Arlington National Cemetery, as well as plentiful opportunities for recreation. You'll also find Old Town, Alexandria, a tony community that developed on land that was annexed back from the capital city in 1846.

# Mount Vernon★★★

*16mi south of DC in Alexandria, VA., via the George Washington Memorial Pkwy. 703-780-2000. www.mountvernon.org. Open daily Apr–Aug 8am–5pm; Mar, Sept & Oct 9am–5pm; Nov–Feb 9am–4pm. $11.*

George Washington didn't tell a lie when he referred to his plantation home, which sits on a grassy slope overlooking the Potomac River, as a "well-resorted tavern." In one year alone, the statesman received 432 visitors at Mount Vernon, where he escaped the stress of public office and enjoyed the life of a successful Virginia planter. Today Mount Vernon is still welcoming guests as America's most-visited historic estate.

### The Gentleman Farmer

Washington considered farming the "most delectable" occupation. "It is honorable," he wrote, "it is amusing, and, with judicious management, it is profitable."

Over the years Washington increased Mount Vernon's holdings to more than 8,000 acres, which were divided into five independent but adjoining farms and worked by some 300 slaves.

## Mount Vernon Time Line

**1674** – King Charles II grants the Mount Vernon property to George's great-grandfather, John Washington.

**1740** – George's father deeds the Potomac property to his son Lawrence, George's elder half-brother. Lawrence renames the 2,500-acre estate Mount Vernon, after a British admiral he had admired while serving in the Royal Navy.

**1752** – When Lawrence dies, the 20-year-old George takes over the management of Mount Vernon, leasing it from Lawrence's widow.

**1759** – Washington marries Martha Dandridge Custis, a widow with two children. To accommodate his new family, Washington redecorates the simple 1.5-story farmhouse at Mount Vernon and adds a full story to it.

**1761** – Lawrence's widow dies, making Washington the legal owner of the estate.

**1773** – Washington begins an ambitious enlargement of Mount Vernon, adding two-story additions to the north and south sides of the house, the piazza on the east, the cupola and the curving colonnades. The project takes almost 15 years to complete.

**1797** – Refusing public demands that he serve a third term as president, Washington retires for a final time to Mount Vernon.

**1799** – Washington dies in his bed at Mount Vernon.

> **Mount Vernon Trail**
>
> Running alongside the George Washington Memorial Parkway, this popular paved biking and walking path leads through wetlands along the Potomac River. Turnouts, particularly south of Old Town, Alexandria, allow you to park and walk—or bike—as far as you like. Bike trail maps are available at the visitor center in Alexandria *(221 King St.; 703-838-4200, www.funside.com).*

## The Mansion

In 1858 the Mount Vernon Ladies Association raised the $200,000 necessary to buy the estate. The mansion's broad, columned piazza is Mount Vernon's hallmark. The Georgian farmhouse is set off by a rust-red roof and curved colonnades that connect the two flanking wings. A frugal man, Washington faced the house with "rusticated board," a wood siding plastered with sand to resemble white stone—which was much more expensive. The décor inside the house reflects Washington's final years there, and many of the furnishings belonged to him.

- **Central Hall** – Pine paneling here is "grained" to resemble mahogany. The hall opens onto four rooms and the piazza. From the piazza, there's a lovely **view**★ of the Potomac River and the distant Maryland shore.

- **Dining Room** – This lavish room, with its ornate woodwork, Palladian windows and marble mantel, was the last addition to the house.

- **Master Bedroom** – Simply furnished, Washington's room contains the mahogany four-poster bed in which he died.

- **Washington's Study** – A narrow back staircase leads down to Washington's first-floor study, which contains his desk and his presidential desk chair, and a terrestrial globe commissioned from a London manufacturer.

## The Grounds

Forty acres of forests and landscaped flower and vegetable gardens occupy the estate's grounds, along with 12 small dependencies. These structures recreate the operations of a self-sufficient estate, from the curing, spinning and laundry houses to the living quarters for overseers and slaves.

- **Burial Sites** – The tombs of George and Martha Washington lie beyond the stables. Beyond an iron grille, the couple's marble sarcophagi are visible within an open vault. Interred in the walls of the vault are 27 other family members.

- **Pioneer Farm** – Located near the wharf, the farm features demonstrations of 18C animal husbandry, crop cultivation and brick making.

# Arlington National Cemetery★★

*On the Arlington side of Memorial Bridge, about 3/4mi from the Lincoln Memorial. 703-607-8000. www.arlingtoncemetery.org. Open Apr–Sept daily 8am–7pm. Rest of the year 8am–5pm.*

Endless rows of gleaming white headstones at Arlington National Cemetery may well bring a tear to your eye. The country's most revered burial ground contains the graves of more than 240,000 military personnel and their dependents. Among those laid to rest in the rolling hills of this 612-acre military cemetery are veterans of every armed conflict in which the US has participated since the Revolutionary War.

At the outbreak of the Civil War, the Union Army took Arlington House *(opposite)* as its Washington headquarters, and military installations were erected around the 1,100-acre estate. With much of the fighting taking place around the capital, the need for burial space soon became evident. In 1864, 200 acres of the estate were designated as a burial ground and Arlington House was claimed by the federal government.

In 1883 the Lee family accepted a financial compensation of $150,000 from the government rather than demanding the restitution of the estate, which by that time contained the remains of some 16,000 war casualties. In that same year, Arlington became the official national cemetery of the US.

**Kennedy Gravesites** – An eternal flame marks the simple grave of President John F. Kennedy (1917–1963). Nearby, the grave of John's younger brother, Robert F. Kennedy (1925–1968), is indicated by a white cross.

**Tomb of the Unknowns** – Located behind the Memorial Amphitheater, this tomb contains the remains of soldiers from each of the two world wars and the Korean War. They symbolize all the men and women who lost their lives in those conflicts as well as in the Vietnam War.

**Changing of the Guard** – Don't miss seeing the precision and skill of the military sentries *(daily in summer on the half-hour; rest of the year daily on the hour)*.

---

**Touring the Cemetery**
The cemetery is situated on hilly land crisscrossed with meandering paved routes. Car traffic is permitted only for disabled visitors and for relatives of persons buried here. If you don't feel up to walking, the Tourmobile shuttle operates within the cemetery and stops at the most popular sights (Kennedy gravesites, Tomb of the Unknowns and Arlington House). Purchase tickets for the tour at the visitor center on Memorial Drive.

# Arlington House, The Robert E. Lee Memorial★

*On the grounds of Arlington National Cemetery. 703-557-0613. www.nps.gov/arho.*
*Open year-round daily 9:30am–4:30pm. Closed Jan 1 & Dec 25.*

Surrounded by the white headstones of Arlington Cemetery, this Greek Revival-style house has known its share of famous occupants. Arlington House was built in 1818 by George Washington Parke Custis (his father, John, was the son of Martha Washington by her first husband). When John Custis died during the Revolution, George and Nelly, the youngest of his four children, were brought to Mount Vernon and raised by the Washingtons. After Martha Washington died in 1802, 21-year-old Geroge Custis constructed Arlington House on a 1,100-acre tract of land his father had left him across from the new federal city.

Enter Robert E. Lee. A distant relative of the Custises, Lee grew up in nearby Alexandria, Virginia, and visited the Custis home often as a boy. In 1831 he married Mary Anna Randolph Custis, the only surviving child of George and Mary Lee, at Arlington House. At the Custises' death, title to the mansion passed to the Lees. During the Civil War, the estate grounds were turned into a national cemetery for the Civil War dead *(see Arlington National Cemetery)*. Today the official Robert E. Lee Memorial, furnished with 19C period and Lee family pieces, commands an exceptional **view★★** of DC.

**Tomb of Pierre L'Enfant** – On the lawn in front of Arlington House is the tomb of the man who designed the original city plan for Washington, DC.

**Iwo Jima Memorial★**
*Just outside Arlington National Cemetery via the Ord and Weitzel Gate.*

This striking sculpture honors all US Marines who have lost their lives in military duty. The statue of six American soldiers raising the Stars and Stripes on Mount Suribachi represents an event that took place in 1945 during the assault on the Japanese-controlled island of Iwo Jima. The capture of this strategically located island is considered one of the Marines' greatest victories of World War II. Based on the Pulitzer Prize-winning war photograph by Joseph Rosenthal, the memorial was designed by Horace W. Peaslee and sculpted by Felix de Weldon.

# Manassas National Battlefield Park★★

*29mi southwest of DC in Manassas, VA. Take I-66 West to Exit 47B (Rte. 234 North). Go through the first traffic light, and the visitor center will be on the right at 6411 Sudley Rd. 703-361-1339. www.nps.gov/mana. Open year-round daily 8:30am–5pm. $3. Visitor center closed Thanksgiving Day & Dec 25.*

When you see these peaceful fields now, it's hard to imagine the brutal battles that were fought on this ground. In fact, the first major land battle of the Civil War took place here on Henry Hill, overlooking a creek call Bull Run.

On the morning of July 21, 1861, the 35,000-man Union Army set out from the capital city under the command of General Irvin McDowell to confront the Confederates at Manassas, a key railroad junction southwest of DC. The men, mostly 90-day volunteers, were feeling cocky; they were sure the Rebels would turn tail at the first shot. And a victory here would pave the way to a march on Richmond, the Confederate capital, and a quick end to the war. Confidence was so high that DC residents even packed picnic lunches and rode out to enjoy the show.

But the show they saw was not what they expected. The plucky Confederates stayed to fight, and the violence that followed shocked spectators and soldiers alike. At first the Union forces had the upper hand, but as Confederate reinforcements arrived, the battle's momentum began to shift. By the end of the day, the Confederates had pushed the Federals back across Bull Run, and McDowell's exhausted troops began to retreat.

An important Confederate victory, the First Battle of Bull Run—with its death toll of 900 young men—also proved to everyone that the war would not end quickly. Indeed, the two armies clashed again thirteen months later on the same ground. This time the Union suffered an even greater defeat, at the hands of General Robert E. Lee.

**Henry Hill Visitor Center** – Houses a museum with displays that set the stage and describe the battle. Here you can see the film, *Manassas: End of Innocence*.

**Walking Tours** – Choose from a 1mi loop of Henry Hill, or two 5mi loops covering the battle grounds of the first (1861) and second (1862) battles at Manassas.

**Driving Tour** – This 13mi, self-guided drive covers 11 key sites of the second battle at Bull Run.

### How "Stonewall" Jackson Got His Name

As things were looking grim for the Confederate Army early in the first Battle of Bull Run, commander Barnard Bee tried to keep the Confederate lines from collapsing. Seeing newly arrived general Thomas J. Jackson sitting tall in the saddle alongside his brigade, Bee shouted: "There stands Jackson like a stone wall! Rally behind the Virginians!"

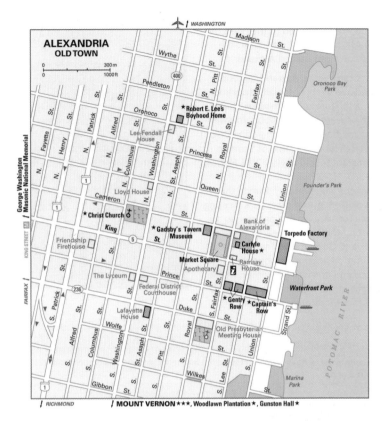

ALEXANDRIA
OLD TOWN

★ Robert E. Lee's Boyhood Home

Lee-Fendall House

★ Christ Church

★ Gadsby's Tavern Museum

Friendship Firehouse

Bank of Alexandria

Torpedo Factory

Carlyle House ★

Market Square

Apothecary

Ramsay House

The Lyceum

Federal District Courthouse

Waterfront Park

★ Gentry Row  ★ Captain's Row

Lafayette House

Old Presbyterian Meeting House

Lloyd House

Marina Park

George Washington Masonic National Memorial

POTOMAC RIVER

Oronoco Bay Park

Founder's Park

/ RICHMOND        / MOUNT VERNON ★★★, Woodlawn Plantation ★, Gunston Hall ★

# Old Town Alexandria★★

*8mi south of DC via the George Washington Memorial Pkwy. Ramsey House Visitor Center is located at 221 King St. 703-838-4200. www.funside.com.*

When you tire of the hustle and bustle of the city, hop on the Metro *(get off at King St.)* and spend a day in Old Town. This walkable, tree-shaded enclave of brick sidewalks, shops, restaurants and 18C architecture on the banks of the Potomac River just oozes Colonial charm and slow-paced Southern gentility.

## Torpedo Factory

*105 N. Union St. 703-838-4565. www.torpedofactory.org.* Art fans won't want to miss Alexandria's extensive visual-arts center. Overlooking the Potomac River, the cavernous building was indeed used to manufacture topedoes during the world wars. Now it houses the studios and shops of more than 150 professional artists and craftspeople.

The area now called Old Town, Alexandria, began with a tobacco warehouse built on the waterfront in the early 1700s. Prominent Scottish tobacco merchants and Virginia tobacco planters petitioned the Virginia General Assembly to establish a town here, and in 1748 the assembly granted their request. The

60-acre tract on which the town was to be sited belonged to members of the Alexander family, and thus the new town was named Alexandria.

In its early years, Alexandria flourished as a lively colonial seaport. It was a mixture of warehouses, shipyards, taverns, small clapboard dwellings and fine Georgian mansions, like **Carlyle House★**, home of Scottish immigrant John Carlyle *(121 N. Fairfax St.; 703-549-2997; www.carlylehouse.org)*. During the Revolution, Alexandria was a meeting place for such leaders as George Mason, who lived at nearby Gunston Hall, and George Washington, whose plantation, Mount Vernon, was located 8mi down the Potomac. At the height of the war, in 1779, Alexandria was incorporated as a town.

### A Day On The Old Town

- Stroll along brick-paved **Gentry Row★** *(200 block of Prince St.)* and cobblestone **Captain's Row★** *(100 block of Prince St.)*, where 18C and 19C town houses recall Alexandria's seafaring days.

- Sample colonial fare at 1770 **Gadsby's Tavern Museum★**, considered in its day to be the finest public house in the new capital *(134 N. Royal St.; museum visit by guided tour only; restaurant open to the public; 703-838-4242; www.gadsbytavern.org)*.

- Browse the shops along **King Street**, Old Town's main commercial thoroughfare. Along the way you'll pass **Market Square** *(between Royal & Fairfax Sts.)*, dominated by the steepled 1873 City Hall.

- Visit venerable **Christ Church★** *(corner of N. Washington & Cameron Sts.; 703-549-1450)*. Both George Washington and Robert E. Lee worshipped in the simple brick and stone 1773 structure. By tradition, 20C presidents worship in Washington's pew on the Sunday nearest his birthday (February 22).

- Walk by **Robert E. Lee's Boyhood Home★** *(607 Oronoco St.; not open to the public)*, where Lee lived when he was young.

### George Washington Masonic National Memorial

*101 Callahan Dr. at the west end of King St. 703-683-2007. www.gwmemorial.org. Open year-round daily 9am–4pm. Closed Jan 1, Thanksgiving Day & Dec 25.*

This memorial to George Washington, the first master of Alexandria's Masonic Lodge, anchors the west end of Old Town. The large granite building, topped by a seven-story tiered tower, is modeled after the lighthouse on the island of Pharos near Alexandria, Egypt. Begun in 1923, the memorial was built in increments over the course of 40 years.

# Great Falls Park ★

*15mi north of DC in McLean, VA. Take the George Washington Memorial Pkwy. North to the exit for I-495 South. Exit on Rte. 193 (Georgetown Pike) and turn right on Old Dominion Dr. Follow Old Dominion about 4.5mi and turn right at sign for Great Falls. 703-285-2965. www.nps.gov/gwmp/grfa. Open year round daily 7am–dusk. $3. Closed Dec 25.*

Great Falls may not be a theme-park ride, but it *is* an awesome series of cascading rapids that drop 76ft in elevation over a distance of less than a mile. Here the waters of the Potomac River gather speed as they narrow from 2,500ft to 60ft and funnel through the jagged cliffs of Mather Gorge.

First identified by an early settler as the "Great Falls of the Potomac," the falls were the site of an amusement park in the early 1900s. The park was a huge success until floods damaged its structures. Later rejected by the Potomac Power Company as unfit for hydroelectric development, the land came into the hands of the National Park Service in 1966. Today the 800-acre park, with its series of 20ft-high falls, provides visitors with a spectacular setting in which to hike, bike, horseback ride, picnic or just enjoy the view.

> ### The Patowmack Canal
>
> George Washington's pet project, the Patowmack Canal was intended to connect the East Coast with the headwaters of the Ohio River, thereby opening a waterway west for trade. In 1784 the Patowmack Company was established to build a canal with a series of locks that would make the Potomac River navigable between Georgetown and the river's headwaters at Cumberland, Maryland. Crews began work in 1786, but roaring rapids, solid rock and plunging falls slowed their progress and the canal took 16 years to complete. Unfortunately, Washington died in 1799, two years before the canal opened at Great Falls.
>
> Although the waterway operated for more than 20 years, in the end the venture was a failure. High construction costs bankrupted the Patowmack Company in 1828, and the canal was eventually abandoned.

**River Trail** – Begins just downstream of the falls and leads along the clifftops for 3mi *(allow 2hrs)*, allowing fantastic views of the roaring whitewater.

**Patowmack Canal Trail** – This 2.5mi trail *(allow 1hr)* passes ruins of the Patowmack Canal, now a Civil Engineering Landmark, en route to the head of the falls.

# Gunston Hall★

*20mi south of DC. Take I-95 South to Exit 163, then follow the signs to Gunston Hall. From Mount Vernon or Woodlawn, continue south on US-1 and turn left on Gunston Rd. (Rte. 242). 703-550-9220. www.gunstonhall.org. Open year-round daily 9:30am–5pm. Closed Jan 1, Thanksgiving Day & Dec 25. $8.*

Sure you've heard of George Washington and Thomas Jefferson, but how about George Mason? If you've read the Constitution of the United States, you've read his words *(see sidebar below)*. Now a relatively obscure patriot, **George Mason** (1725–1792) in his day was a respected thinker whose writings influenced the course of the Revolution and the development of the young Republic.

In 1755 Mason began constructing his Georgian manor house on the Virginia shoreline about a mile above the Potomac—not far from Mount Vernon. With its large symmetrical chimneys and plain brick facade, Gunston Hall reflects the style of plantation life favored by wealthy 18C Virginia planters.

As young men, Mason and George Washington developed a friendship, and over the years they frequently exchanged views about the development of the new nation. Though he served as a member of the Virginia House of Burgesses and a delegate to the Constitutional Convention of 1787, Mason preferred to exercise his influence quietly, through writings and private conversations. He died at Gunston Hall in 1792, just as the young Republic was being formed. Two raised sarcophagi on the estate grounds contain the remains of George Mason and his wife, Ann.

---

### What's Inside the Mansion?

- The interior of the house is noted for its mid-18C carved **woodwork** by English craftsman William Buckland.

- The **Chinese formal parlor** is the only surviving room in America featuring the scalloped Chinoiserie woodworking of the colonial period.

- English Palladian-style woodwork decorates the **dining room**.

---

### Let Freedom Ring

"That all men are born equally free and independent and have certain inherent natural Rights . . . among which are the Enjoyment of Life and Liberty, with the Means of acquiring and possessing Property, and pursuing and obtaining Happiness and Safety."

Sound familiar? It should. These words from the first draft of the Virginia Declaration of Rights, penned by George Mason in May 1776, were echoed by Mason's friend Thomas Jefferson in his draft of the Declaration of Independence (July 1776).

# Woodlawn Plantation★

*19mi south of DC. Take the George Washington Memorial Pkwy. south to Rte. 235 South to Rte. 1 South. 9000 Richmond Hwy. (Rte. 1), Alexandria, VA. 703-780-4000. www.wood lawnplantation.org. Visit by guided tour only year-round daily 10am–5pm. Closed Jan, Feb, Thanksgiving Day & Dec 25. $7.50; combination ticket with Pope-Leighey House $13.50.*

It's good to have relatives in high places. That was certainly the case for Lawrence Lewis and Eleanor "Nelly" Custis Lewis, favored relatives of President George Washington and his wife, Martha (Lawrence was George's nephew; Nelly was Martha's granddaughter). As a wedding gift, Washington gave the couple a 2,000-acre tract west of Mount Vernon. He also deeded them a nearby mill and distillery, because, as he advised Lawrence, "a young man should have objects of employment. Idleness is disreputable." In 1802 the Lewises moved into the completed north wing of the house.

After Lawrence died in 1839, Nelly went to live with her son in Clark County. Seven years later, the family offered Woodlawn at public sale. The estate knew several different owners before it became the property of the National Trust for Historic Preservation in 1957.

**The Mansion** – Designed by prominent architect Dr. William Thornton, this Georgian brick mansion incorporates two symmetrical one-and-a-half-story wings connected to the main house by one-story covered walkways known as "hyphens." Inside, the house contains many of the furnishings that belonged to the family, including several pieces that were brought from Mount Vernon.

### Pope-Leighey House

*On the grounds of Woodlawn, below the parking lot. 703-780-4000. Same hours as Woodlawn.* The claim to fame of this small, L-shaped house is that it was designed by renowned 20C architect Frank Lloyd Wright. Built in 1941 for Loren Pope, a journalist in nearby Falls Church, Virginia, the 1,200sq ft, five-room house cost roughly $7,000. Now owned by the National Trust for Historic Preservation, which moved the structure to Woodlawn, the residence contains the furniture that Wright designed for it. Only cypress, brick, glass and concrete were used to build the house, according to Wright's practice of using as few materials as possible.

**T**ired of trekking to museums and monuments in the nation's capital? Within two and a half hours, you can drive away from the city to nearby Virginia, West Virginia, Maryland and Pennsylvania. Each of these areas has its own charms, whether you prefer to discover the history of Harpers Ferry or Colonial Williamsburg, go bird-watching on Maryland's Eastern Shore, or visit the grand du Pont estates and gardens in Pennsylvania's Brandywine Valley.

## Colonial Williamsburg★★★

*151mi southeast of DC via I-95 South to I-64 East. 757-229-1000. www.colonialwilliamsburg.org. Open year-round daily 9am–5pm. Hours vary at certain buildings & tradeshops. $39.*

You'll think you've landed back in the 18C as you walk the streets of this painstakingly re-created 301-acre town site. Here you'll encounter costumed guides and character interpreters depicting citizens of Virginia's 18C colonial capital going about their daily routines. Just don't expect these well-versed actors to break character—they're firmly entrenched in the 18C.

Williamsburg's roots date to 1699, when colonial legislators decided to move their capital from Jamestown inland to Middle Plantation, where the **College of William and Mary**★ *(west end of Duke of Gloucester St.; 757-221-4000; www.wm.edu)* had been recently founded. The new capital, named after England's King William III, centered around mile-long, unpaved Duke of Gloucester Street, anchored on the east by the colonial capitol and on the west by the college. The town rapidly grew into an important governmental center. From Virginia's House of Burgesses came some of the leading figures of the American Revolution—Peyton Randolph, George Washington, Thomas Jefferson and Patrick Henry. In 1780 the Virginia capital was moved to Richmond.

### Tips For Visiting

The best way to decipher Williamsburg is to begin at the Visitor Center *(Lafayette St. near the intersection with the Colonial Pkwy.)*, where you can purchase several different types of passes that encompass varying amounts of time and numbers of sights. Many buildings, including the Capitol and Governor's Palace, are open by guided tour only. Historic homes are open on different days of the week; check when you buy your ticket. Before you start exploring, get a grounding in the town's history by watching the 35-minute film, *Williamsburg: The Story of a Patriot.*

Williamsburg languished until 1926, when John D. Rockefeller Jr. provided the funding for scholars and archaeologists to began reconstructing the colonial town. Today, Colonial Williamsburg includes 88 original shops, houses and public buildings and hundreds of reconstructed colonial structures on their original sites.

**Capitol**★★★ – *East end of Duke of Gloucester St.* Originally completed in 1705 (the current building is a reconstruction), the Capitol's H shape symbolizes the bicameral system of British colonial government. Elected burgesses sat on the sparely decorated east side of the building, and the royal governor and his council convened on the ornate west side.

**Raleigh Tavern**★★ – *Duke of Gloucester St., one block west of the capitol.* In its heyday, Raleigh Tavern stood at the pivot of the capital's social life, welcoming regulars George Washington, Thomas Jefferson and Peyton Randolph.

**Governor's Palace**★★★ – *North end of Palace Green.* With its elegant woodwork, period furnishings and an incomparable ornamental display of 18C firearms, this reconstruction of the 1722 royal governor's palace was the most impressive building of its era in the colonies. Kids will love the **boxwood maze** that lies behind the palace.

**George Wythe House**★★ – *West side of Palace Green.* This original 18C Georgian brick residence was home to George Wythe (1726–1806), Virginia's most respected jurist and the College of William and Mary's first law professor.

**DeWitt Wallace Gallery**★★ – *S. Henry & Francis Sts. 757-220-7554.* Located on the lower level of the historic Public Hospital, the gallery is renowned for its collection of English and American pieces dating from 1600 to 1830.

**Abby Aldrich Rockefeller Folk Art Center**★★ – *On S. England St., next to the Williamsburg Inn. 757-220-7670. www.colonialwilliamsburg.org.* Named for the wife of John D. Rockefeller Jr., the center boasts one of the finest collections of American folk art in the world.

### Colonial Williamsburg After Hours

After the crowds have left, nighttime is one of the best times to experience Colonial Williamsburg. More than 27 houses and taverns here have overnight guest rooms for rent *(757-229-1000)*. All are decorated with reproduction antiques and offer the ambience of the past with the comforts of the present. Be sure to have dinner *(reserve well in advance; 757-229-1000)* at one of the four colonial taverns—King's Arms, Christiana Campbell's, Shields, Josiah Chowning's—where you'll be entertained by 18C storytellers and balladeers. After dinner, go for "Gambols" (colonial card games) at Josiah Chowning's Tavern *(Duke of Gloucester St.).*

# Monticello★★★

*125mi southwest of DC. Take I-66 West to US-29 South to Charlottesville. Follow Rte. 250 West/29 Bypass South to I-64 East; turn left on Rte. 53 and follow signs. 434-984-9822. www.monticello.org. Open Mar–Oct daily 8am–5pm, Nov–Feb daily 9am–4:30pm. Closed Dec 25. $13.*

Thomas Jefferson seemingly never did anything halfway. The home that Jefferson designed for himself outside Charlottesville, Virginia now ranks as the only house in the US on the UNESCO World Heritage List of international treasures. Best known as the author of the Declaration of Independence, Jefferson held positions including governor of Virginia, minister to France, secretary of State, vice president and third US president (1801-09).

> ### Michie Tavern★
>
> *683 Thomas Jefferson Pkwy. 434-977-1234. www.michietavern.com.* On your way up the mountain to Monticello stop at Michie Tavern (established in 1784) for a trip back in time. Inside the rambling white structure you can feast colonial-style on the "ordinary," a set midday meal of fried chicken, stewed tomatoes, black-eyed peas, biscuits and cornbread.

Jefferson, an accomplished draftsman, musician and naturalist, began building his home in 1768 on the little mountain ("Monticello") that still commands fine views of the countryside. Upon returning from a five-year assignment as minister to France in 1796, Jefferson enlarged the house from 8 to 21 rooms and crowned the west entrance with a dome.

**Visit** – At the visitor center at the base of the mountain *(Rte. 20, just south of I-64, Exit 121; 434-977-1783)* you can view an introductory film, after which trams take you up to the house. Tours begin in the entrance hall, which Jefferson used as a museum. Inside, you'll see thoughtful innovations at every turn, from heat-conserving double doors to skylights and a dumbwaiter. After the tour, be sure to explore the all-weather passageway underneath the house, leading to the wine cellar and kitchen.

## Charlottesville★★

*125mi southwest of DC via I-66 West to US-29 South. Tourist information: 434-293-6789 or www.charlottesvilletourism.org.*

Set amid the eastern foothills of the Blue Ridge Mountains and surrounded by the lush horse farms of Albemarle County, this university town was founded as the county seat in 1762. Well removed from Virginia's more established aristocracy, the area fostered a tough self-reliance that would produce several state and national leaders, including three of the country's first five presidents— Thomas Jefferson (1801–09), James Madison (1809–17) and James Monroe (1817–25). In addition to Jefferson's Monticello, **Ash Lawn-Highland**★ *(Rte. 53, east of Rte. 20; 434-293-9539; http://avenue.org/ashlawn)* preserves the remains of Monroe's tobacco plantation, and **Montpelier**★★ *(24mi northeast of Charlottesville via Rte. 20; 540-672-2728; www.montpelier.org)* gives visitors a look at Madison's former estate.

### Where To Stay

**Boar's Head Inn**
*200 Ednam Dr., off Rte. 250 West, Charlottesville, VA. 434-296-2181 or 800-476-1988. www.boarsheadinn.com. 171 rooms. $125–$200.* This 573-acre estate offers 20 tennis courts, 4 pools, a golf course, a fitness facility and a full-service spa. Seventeenth-century antiques create a pub-like feel in the common areas, while spacious guest rooms feature four-poster beds and damask duvets. Of the inn's four restaurants, the **Old Mill Room** offers award-winning fine dining.

**Keswick Hall**
*701 Club Dr., Keswick, VA. 434-979-3440 or 800-274-5391. www.keswick.com. 48 rooms. Over $200.* You'll think you're on an English country estate when you arrive at stately Keswick Hall. Located just minutes from Monticello, the Italianate mansion sports Laura Ashley fabrics and wall coverings. An 18-hole Arnold Palmer golf course lies at your doorstep, along with swimming, tennis and spa treatments. The **dining room** serves memorable regional American cuisine that changes with the season.

## University of Virginia★★

*US-29 & US-250 Business (Emmet St. & University Ave.), Charlottesville. 434-924-7969. www.virginia.edu.*

Thomas Jefferson's retirement project, the University of Virginia is a carefully planned "academical village" and one of only four works of architecture in the country to be included on the UNESCO World Heritage List. Today the university, which began in 1817, enrolls some 18,000 students and ranks as one of the top universities in the eastern US.

The heart of Jefferson's village, the graceful **Rotunda**★★★ *(University Ave. & Rugby Rd.)*, completed in 1826, was patterned on the Pantheon in Rome. Stand on the south Rotunda steps where you'll have a sweeping view of the **Lawn**, flanked by colonnades that link student rooms with ten pavilions. Each pavilion is modelled after a different Greek or Roman temple and is occupied by university deans and distinguished professors.

# Annapolis★★

*31mi east of DC via US-50 East. 410-280-0445. www.visit-annapolis.org.*

You can easily spend a day in Annapolis, Maryland drooling over the yachts tied up at the City Dock, poking around in the boutiques that crowd the surrounding blocks, and ogling the Naval Academy cadets in their crisp uniforms. But don't stop there—take some time to discover the rich history of this small city.

Established on the banks of the Severn River by Virginia Puritans in 1648, Annapolis became the seat of colonial government in 1694, and subsequently grew to be a busy port. The city's 1779 redbrick **State House★** *(center of State Circle; 410-974-3400)* served as the US capitol between 1783 and 1784. It was here, on January 14, 1784, that the Continental Congress ratified the Treaty of Paris, officially ending the Revolutionary War.

• **Hammond Harwood House★★** *(19 Maryland Ave.; 410-263-4683; www.hammondharwoodhouse.org)*, built by William Buckland in 1775, and **Chase-Lloyd House★** *(22 Maryland Ave.; 410-263-2723)*, known for its split, cantilevered staircase, typify the elegant Georgian-style residences built in Annapolis in the 18C.

**United States Naval Academy★** – *Armel-Leftwich Visitor Center, 52 King George St. 410-263-6933. www.navyonline.com.*

Future officers in the US Navy and Marine Corps study on this peaceful, 338-acre campus established in 1845 along the Severn River and Spa Creek. The guided walking tour *(depart from the visitor center, inside Gate 1 on King George St.)* around "the Yard," as the academy grounds are called, includes **Bancroft Hall**, the 1906 Baroque structure in the center of campus that covers 27 acres and boasts 5mi of corridors. The tour also stops at the copper-domed **Navy Chapel★★**, modeled after the Hôtel des Invalides in Paris.

Before you leave, check out the **U.S. Naval Academy Museum** in Preble Hall, where you'll find a rare collection of 17C to 19C **ship models★★** made in England, as well as other artifacts detailing the history of the Navy.

## Baltimore's Inner Harbor★★

*38mi northeast of DC. Take I-95 North to Exit 27 and continue north to Baltimore. Take Exit 53 onto I-395 and follow it until it ends; turn right on Conway St. to the Inner Harbor. 410-659-730. www.southbaltimore.com/innerharbor.*

No matter what your age, you're bound to enjoy this glittering waterfront complex of shops, restaurants, museums and hotels *(bounded by Pratt & Light Sts.)*. Rescued from its downtrodden state in the 1960s, Baltimore's harbor is now anchored on the northeast and southwest corners by the National Aquarium and the **Maryland Science Center** *(601 Light St.; 410-685-5225; www.mdsci.org)* respectively. In between, the twin glass pavilions of **Harborplace** overlook the brick pier where the 1854 "sloop-of-war" USS *Constellation* is docked and open for tours *(410-539-1797; www.constellation.org)*. Inside Harborplace's pavilions you'll find a festival of shops and eateries.

• **Camden Yards** – The city's beloved Orioles play baseball a few blocks west of the waterfront *(333 W. Camden St.; 410-547-6234; www.oriolestickets.net)*.

**National Aquarium in Baltimore★★** – *Pier Three, 501 E. Pratt St. 410-576-3800. www.aqua.org. Open Mar–Jun & Sept–Oct daily 9am–7pm (Fri until 8pm). Jul–Aug Sun–Thu 9am–8pm, Fri & Sat 9am–10pm. Closed Thanksgiving & Dec 25. $17.50.*

More than 10,000 marine creatures occupy the habitats within Baltimore's star attraction. In the five-story Main Aquarium you can see the country's largest collection of rays in **Wings in the Water★**, and walk down through four stories of sharks, corals and other reef denizens in the **Atlantic Coral Reef★**. Save time for the dolphin show that takes place in the adjoining Marine Mammal Pavilion *(showtimes are assigned when you buy an admission ticket)*.

**Baltimore Maritime Museum★** – *Ticket booth on Pier Three next to the aquarium. 410-396-3853. www.baltomaritimemuseum.org. Open year-round daily at 10am. Closing hours vary according to season. $7.*

This partially floating museum consists of four sites—three historic vessels and the **Seven Foot Knoll Lighthouse**—that are linked by the Inner Harbor.

# Brandywine Valley ★★

*120mi north of DC via I-95 North to Wilmington, Delaware. 610-280-6145.*
*www.brandywinevalley.com.*

As narrow Brandywine Creek (locally known as the Brandywine River) weaves its way through Chester County, Pennsylvania, and into Delaware, it creates in its wake a valley so charming that you just have to see it for yourself. The natural beauty of the Brandywine Valley has spurred wealthy industrialists to build elaborate mansions on its hillsides and inspired artists to capture its green countryside on canvas.

Back in the early 19C, French immigrant **Eleuthère Irénée (E.I.) du Pont** was drawn to the valley for a more practical reason. Realizing the river's potential as a source of hydroelectric power, he established a black-powder mill on the banks of the Brandywine. Today **Hagley Museum**★★ *(on Rte. 141 between Rtes. 100 & US-202 in Wilmington, DE; 302-658-2400; www.hagley.lib.de.us; open mid-May–Dec daily 9:30am–4:30pm; $7.50)* preserves du Pont's mill complex, which in its heyday was the world's largest producer of black powder.

**Longwood Gardens**★★★ – *Located off US-1 just west of Rte. 52 near Kennett Square, PA. 610-388-1000. www.longwoodgardens.org. Open year-round daily 9am–5pm. Closing hours vary according to season. $12–$15, depending on tour.*

Eleuthère's great-grandson Pierre S. du Pont (1870–1954) created this world-renowned 1,050-acre horticultural masterpiece—despite a demanding career as chairman of the board of both DuPont and General Motors. Gardeners of all ages will be delighted by the **Italian Water Garden**★★, the enormous Beaux-Arts **Conservatory**★★★ and du Pont's Main Fountain Garden, where 380 fountainheads, colored lights and music create a spectacular **Festival of Fountains**★★ on summer evenings.

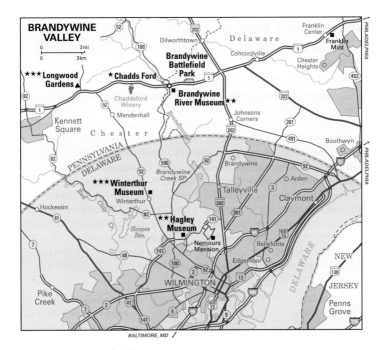

BALTIMORE, MD

**Winterthur Museum**★★★ – *On Rte. 52, 5mi south of US-1, in Winterthur, DE. 302-888-4600. www.winterthur.org. Open year-round daily 10am–5pm. $20.*

Henry Francis du Pont (1880–1969) liked to collect things—pieces of American decorative art to be exact. His unsurpassed **decorative-arts collection**★★★ is showcased in 175 re-created **period rooms**★★★ that fill Winterthur mansion (c.1830s), which sits on 965 acres on the outskirts of Wilmington, Delaware. Consisting of more than 89,000 objects, the collection represents the best in American porcelain, furniture, pewter and silver, and portraiture from 1640 to 1860.

**Brandywine River Museum**★★ – *On US-1, just south of intersection with Rte. 100, in Chadds Ford, PA. 610-388-2700. www.brandywinemuseum.org. Open year-round daily 9:30am–4:30pm. Closed Dec 25. $6.*

This Civil War-era gristmill on the banks of the Brandywine River is now a museum justly famous for its collection of paintings by members of the **Wyeth** family: illustrator Newell Convers (N.C.) Wyeth (1882–1945), his son Andrew (b. 1917), and Andrew's son Jamie (b. 1946).

**Nemours Mansion**★ – *1600 Rockland Rd., off Rte. 141, Wilmington, DE. 302-651-6912. www.nemours.org. Visit by guided tour only Tue–Sat 9am, 11am, 1pm & 3pm; Sun 11am, 1pm & 3pm. Closed Mon & Dec–Apr. Visitors must be over 12 years of age. $10.*

You can't say that the du Ponts didn't live in high style. This 102-room, Louis XVI-style chateau belonged to industrialist and philanthropist Alfred I. du Pont (1864–1935). Completed in 1910, Nemours brims with period antiques, crystal chandeliers (including one owned by the Marquis de Lafayette) and priceless artwork. The 300-acre estate, named for the family's ancestral home in France, also boasts some of the finest formal French-style **gardens** in the US.

# Harpers Ferry National Historic Park★★

*55mi northwest of DC in Harpers Ferry, West Virginia. From DC, take I-270 North to Frederick, Maryland, then go south on US-340. 304-535-6223. www.nps.gov/hafe. Open year-round daily 8am–5pm. Closed Jan 1, Thanksgiving Day & Dec 25. $5.*

You may not know that this tiny West Virginia town takes its name from builder Robert Harper, who settled at the junction of the Shenandoah and Potomac rivers in 1751. You've more likely heard Harpers Ferry associated with abolitionist **John Brown** (1800–1859). In 1859 Brown led a 21-man "army of the liberation" into town, planning to sieze weapons from the US Armory and Arsenal in Harpers Ferry to use in waging a guerrilla war against slavery from the nearby mountains. When federal troops arrived to stop the raid, Brown and some of his followers barricaded themselves in the brick fire-engine/guard house. On October 18, a storming party of Marines broke into Brown's "fort" and captured the raiders. Brown was tried and convicted of "conspiring with slaves to commit treason and murder." He was hanged in December 1859. Although Brown's raid failed, the incident inflamed tensions between the North and South and set the stage for a series of events that erupted two years later in the Civil War.

**Information Center** – *Shenandoah St.* Here you can see exhibits outlining the town's history and pick up a copy of the *Lower Town Trail Guide* to 24 key historic sites clustered on narrow, hilly Shenandoah, High and Potomac streets. From Jefferson Rock, you'll enjoy the same view that Thomas Jefferson described in 1783 as being "worth a voyage across the Atlantic." When you're ready for a break from sightseeing, tackle the many shops that line High Street.

---

### Wild, Wonderful West Virginia

With its location at the confluence of the Shenandoah and Potomac rivers, Harpers Ferry provides a great base for many a watery adventure. Canoeing, kayaking, whitewater rafting and tubing trips all begin here. For information, contact one of these local outfitters:

**Blue Ridge Outfitters** – *304-725-3444; www.broraft.com.*

**Historical River Tours** – *410-489-2837; www.historicalrivertours.com.*

**River Riders** – *304-535-2663; www.riverriders.com.*

For landlubbers, the 2,000mi-long **Appalachian Trail** also runs through Harpers Ferry. In fact, the Appalachian Trail Conference Information Center is located right in town *(799 Washington St.; 304-535-6331; www.appalachiantrail.org).*

## Skyline Drive★★

*70mi west of DC via I-66. 540-999-3500. www.nps.gov/shen. Open year-round daily. $5.*

If you like scenic mountain drives, you'll love this one. Skyline Drive, the best-known feature within the more than 196,030 acres of **Shenandoah National Park★★**, traces the backbone of the Blue Ridge for 105mi as it runs through western Virginia. Girdled by low stone walls, 75 parking overlooks along the drive offer one dazzling view after another. To the east, the Piedmont's gentle, rounded hills slope down into the coastal plain. The western peaks give way to the Shenandoah Valley, named for the river that winds lazily past fields, woods and farms. At Rockfish Gap, Virginia, Skyline Drive hooks up seamlessly with the **Blue Ridge Parkway★★** and continues south through North Carolina. The parkway ends in Cherokee near the entrance to **Great Smoky Mountains National Park★★★** *(865-436-1200; www.nsp.gov/grsm).*

*Skyline Drive begins at US-340 at the south edge of Front Royal, Virginia.*

**Skyline Caverns** – *1mi south of park entrance on US-340, Front Royal, VA. 540-636-4545. www.skylinecaverns.com.* This 60-million-year-old limestone cave includes **Fairyland Lake★**, whose glassy surface shimmers in the glow of multicolored lights.

**Front Royal to Thornton Gap** – *31.5mi.* Skyline Drive climbs to **Shenandoah Valley Overlook** *(mile 2.8)*, where the sweeping **view★★** west takes in Massanutten Mountain. **Hogwallow Flats Overlook** *(mile 13.8)* looks east over lumpy peaks called monadnocks, remnants of a range that predates the Blue Ridge.

> ### Visiting Shenandoah National Park
>
> The park is open year-round, though portions of Skyline Drive may be temporarily closed in winter due to weather conditions. Many of the park facilities are closed from late November through March.
>
> The speed limit in the park is 35mph. Concrete mile markers located on the west side of the road are numbered in increasing order from north to south.
>
> More than 500mi of trails thread through the park, including 101mi of the **Appalachian Trail** (which runs from Maine to Georgia). Maps, information and free back-country permits are available at the park headquarters in Luray, VA *(540-999-3500)* and at the park's three visitor centers: Dickey Ridge *(mile 4.6)*, Harry F. Byrd *(mile 51)*, and Loft Mountain *(mile 79.5)*.

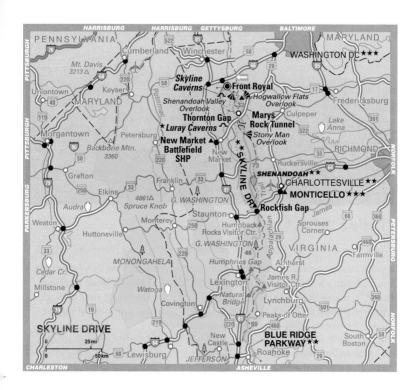

**Luray Caverns**★ – *9mi west of Thornton Gap Entrance on US-211, Luray, VA. 540-743-6551. www.luraycaverns.com.* Lying some 160ft underground, popular Luray Caverns shimmers with stalactites and flowstone that drips from the ceiling.

**New Market Battlefield State Historical Park** – *21mi west of Thornton Gap entrance on US-211, New Market, VA. 540-740-3101. www4.vmi.edu/museum.* On these bucolic pastures west of the Blue Ridge, 257 cadets from the Virginia Military Institute in Lexington helped defeat Union forces in May 1864.

**Marys Rock Tunnel to Rockfish Entrance Station**★★ – *73mi.* To create the short length of Marys Rock Tunnel *(mile 32.4),* workers drilled through more than 600ft of rock for three months before the tunnel opened to traffic in 1932. From **Stony Man Overlook** *(mile 38.6)* you can see Old Rag, crowned in one-billion-year-old granite.

*Skyline Drive ends at Rockfish Gap (mile 105.4), where two major east-west highways, US-250 and I-64, cross the mountains.*

**Frontier Culture Museum**★★ – *5mi west of I-81 Exit 222 off US-250 West in Staunton, VA. 540-332-7850. www.frontiermuseum.org. Open mid-Mar–Nov daily 9am–5pm. Rest of the year 10am–4pm. Closed Thanksgiving, Dec 25 & Jan 1. $10.* Nestled in the farmlands of the Shenandoah Valley, this 78-acre outdoor living-history complex preserves the region's European heritage through a series of 17C to 19C farm buildings that were dismantled and moved to this site.

## Maryland's Eastern Shore ★

*50mi east of DC via US-50 East across the Chesapeake Bay Bridge. 410-767-3400 or 800-634-7386. www.mdisfun.org.*

Think sleepy fishing villages, small farms, and a low-lying coastline cut by quiet coves and lonely marshes. This is Maryland's Eastern Shore, a peninsula that lies between the Chesapeake Bay and the Atlantic Ocean, just across the Bay Bridge from Annapolis. You can easily while away a couple of pleasant days here exploring historic waterside villages such as **St. Michaels ★** and **Chestertown**, staying in some of the fine bed-and-breakfast inns, bird-watching and poking through myriad antique shops. And while you're there, be sure to sample the region's bountiful seafood—especially the Chesapeake Bay's famous blue crabs *(in season Jun–Oct)*.

**Pony Penning ★** – One of the shore's most unique events takes place each summer on the southern end of **Assateague Island National Seashore ★** *(29mi east of Salisbury, MD, via US-50 & Rte. 611; 410-641-1441; www.nps.gov/asis).* This part of the 37mi-long barrier island harbors several hundred wild ponies that roam **Chincoteague National Wildlife Refuge** across the Maryland state line in Virginia. The offspring of horses brought here by 17C European settlers to avoid taxes, the ponies are rounded up annually on Assateague Island and herded across the narrow channel (at slack tide) to the town of Chincoteague *(across Chincoteague Bay on Rte. 175).* Here the annual Pony Penning, the public roundup and sale of foals, is held on the last Wednesday and Thursday of July *(for details, call 757-336-6161 or check online at www.chincoteaguechamber.com).*

### Inn at Perry Cabin

*308 Watkins Lane, St. Michaels, MD. 78mi east of DC via US-50 East. 410-745-2200 or 800-722-2949. www.perrycabin.com. 81 rooms. Over $200.*

This lovely white Colonial mansion was built on the banks of the Miles River just after the War of 1812 by Samuel Hambleton, aide-de-camp to Commodore Oliver Hazard Perry. Take a dip in the heated pool, borrow one of the inn's bikes and cycle around historic St. Michaels, or schedule a sailing trip or a fishing charter. At the end of the day, come back to relax in rooms decked out in English and early American antiques and Laura Ashley prints. The innovative American cuisine at **Sherwood's Landing** incorporates fresh local seafood.

*The venues listed below were selected for their ambience, location and/or value for money. Rates indicate the average cost of an appetizer, an entrée and a dessert for one person (not including tax, gratuity or beverages). Most restaurants are open daily and accept major credit cards. Call for information regarding reservations, dress code and opening hours. Restaurants listed are located in Washington, DC, unless otherwise noted. For a complete listing of restaurants mentioned in this guide, see Index.*

| | | |
|---|---|---|
| **$$$$** over $50 | **$$** $15–$30 | |
| **$$$** $30–$50 | **$** less than $15 | |

## Luxury

### The Caucus Room                                    $$$$   American

*401 9th St. NW. Closed Sun. 202-393-1300. www.thecaucusroom.com.*

This is the consummate Washington steakhouse, where power players sink into the dark wooded interior and enjoy a tender steak and a glass of merlot. Truly a bipartisan venture, The Caucus Room is partially owned by notable Republican Haley Barbour and Democrat Tom Boggs and boasts a colorful William Woodward mural of a jovial donkey and elephant amicably enjoying a lavish feast. Generous portions and impeccable service justify the high prices.

### Citronelle                                    $$$$   California French

*300 M. St. NW. Closed Sun in July & Aug. 202-625-2150. www.citronelledc.com.*

Located in Georgetown's Latham Hotel, Citronelle brings the inspired innovative cuisine of Michel Richard to DC from the West Coast. Nightly prix-fixe menus range from three courses for $75 to the elaborate eight-course Michel Menu for $120. On any given night your choices might include a starter of escargots or artichoke terrine, and entrées ranging from black bass Barigoule to cote de boeuf with shallot sauce. Housemade petits fours appear at the end of every dinner. *Jackets required.*

## DC Coast

$$$$  New American

*1401 K St. NW. 202-216-5988. Closed Sun. www.dccoast.com.*

A towering bronze mermaid sculpture greets hungry locals at this downtown hotspot. Housed in an Art Deco-era bank, the contemporary dining room features lantern-style chandeliers, oversized oval mirrors and spiral-shaped booths. Chef Jeff Tunks' tri-coastal specialties (Mid-Atlantic, Gulf and West) include tuna tartare chunks with lime and coconut milk, and pan-roasted wild rockfish with crispy polenta cake in lobster corn broth.

## Galileo

$$$$  Northern Italian

*1110 21st St. NW. 202-293-7191. www.robertodonna.com.*

An embarrassment of riches awaits you at Roberto Donna's DC flagship restaurant. Riches here refer to the sumptuous cuisine of Donna's native Piemonte region of Italy. You'll find it difficult to narrow down your choices from the extensive—and mouth-watering—menu. Fragrant bagna cauda (a hot dip made from olive oil, garlic and anchovies) is served with veggies for dipping; risotto is prepared to order; and egg pasta is made on the premises with an artery-hardening 42 egg yolks per two pounds of flour. In summer, when white truffles are in season, treat yourself to the special menu featuring this delicacy in every one of five courses.

## Nora

$$$$  New American

*2132 Florida Ave. NW. Dinner only. Closed Sun. 202-462-5143. www.noras.com.*

America's first certified organic restaurant, Nora is housed in a 19C grocery store in Dupont Circle. Nora Pouillon's politically correct, New American menu (think roasted heirloom-tomato soup and pan-roasted Maine lobster with saffron risotto and pesto) sits well with Washington diners, who have praised her innovative organic creations for 22 years. The fare at Nora's sister restaurant, **Asia Nora $$$** *(2213 M St. NW; 202-797-4860)* shines with intriguing Asian accents.

## Moderate

### Butterfield 9

$$$   New American

*600 14th St. NW. 202-289-8810. www.butterfield9.com.*

Evoking the subtle glamour of black-and-white Hollywood, Butterfield 9's creative American menu skillfully combines retro and modern flavors. Start with gnocchi laced with flavorful truffles or a delicate napoleon of red and golden beets layered with piquant cheeses. From there, move on to a traditional filet mignon or an inventive horseradish-crusted halibut with leek fondue, before feasting on the restaurant's updated version of baked Alaska for dessert.

### Café Atlantico

$$$   Latin American

*405 8th St. NW. 202-393-0812. www.cafeatlanticodc.com.*

Café Atlantico is widely considered conservative Washington's most daring restaurant. Lively and unconventional, chef Katsuya Sukushima tastefully modifies Nuevo Latino flavors to suit Washington's conservative and liberal taste buds. Updated favorites, such as tuna and coconut ceviche, and conch fritters with a liquid heart are suitably paired with refreshing rum-based mojitos or cachaça-infused caipirinhas that really pack a punch.

### District ChopHouse

$$$   American

*509 7th St. NW. 202-347-3434. www.districtchophouse.com.*

Carved out of an old bank building, the District ChopHouse serves what you would expect—thick steaks and smooth beers. Classics like filet mignon, New York strip and Iowa pork chops come with a house salad and choice of starch. On the mezzanine level, a full-service scotch and bourbon bar caters to power brokers, who often get a game going at the hand-carved billiard tables before having a smoke in the cigar lounge.

### Georgia Brown's

$$$   Southern

*950 15th St. NW. 202-393-4499. www.gbrowns.com.*

Locals love this well-appointed downtown eatery for its Lowcountry dishes, which take Southern regional ingredients to new heights. For starters, try the she-crab soup or cornmeal-crusted catfish fingers, then chow down on the likes of Charleston Perlau (red rice mixed with andouille sausage and duck, topped with "heads-on" shrimp) or Southern fried chicken. Selections such as sautéed black-eyed pea cakes appeal to vegetarians.

### Jaleo

$$$   Spanish

*480 7th St. NW. 202-628-7949. www.jaleo.com.*

Trendsetting and always crowded, Jaleo specializes in classic hot and cold Spanish tapas, or small plates, including the restaurant's acclaimed fried calamari with aioli, grilled chorizo and savory steamed mussels. A sure bet is one of the signature paellas, made with Calasparra rice, considered the best in Spain. Unique paella combinations here include lobster and chicken, wild mushroom and chicken, squid and monkfish, and even a vegetarian version. On Wednesday nights, Flamenco dancers weave their sultry way around the tables.

### Jeffrey's                                      $$$   Southwestern

*2650 Virginia Ave. NW. 202-298-4455. www.thewatergatehotel.com.*

Opened in April 2001 in the infamous Watergate Hotel, Jeffrey's accompanied President George W. Bush and Laura Bush to Washington, DC from Austin, Texas. David Garrido's contemporary Texas menu was a Bush favorite, and the couple has been known to sneak out for a quick bite at the new DC location in the notorious Watergate complex. Start with the crispy gulf oysters on yucca root chips, then move on to a tender Texas beef tenderloin.

### Kinkead's                                     $$$   New American

*2000 Pennsylvania Ave. NW. 202-296-7700. www.kinkeads.com.*

Chef Bob Kinkead's award-winning American brasserie focuses on fresh sea-food. Cod with crab Imperial, Virginia ham and cheddar-cheese spoonbread; seared sea scallops with carmelized fennel tart tatin; and softshell crabs with garlic flan are just some of the delights you might find on the daily changing menu here. Braised lamb shanks and grilled rib eye will please serious meat-lovers. Save room for such goodies as chocolate dacquoise napped with cappuccino sauce or key-lime custard cake topped with tropical fruit salsa.

### The Occidental Grill                          $$$   American

*1475 Pennsylvania Ave. NW. 202-783-1475. www.occidentaldc.com.*

 One of Washington's most historic restaurants, the Occidental cozies up against the stately Willard Hotel, near the White House. The classic American menu features a simple, tasty selection of grilled meats and fish with cameo appearances by a trendier Chilean sea bass and marinated veal cheeks.

### Red Sage                                      $$$ Southwestern

*605 14 St. NW. Closed Sun. 202-638-4444. www.redsage.com.*

This two-story restaurant has roped in crowds with its Southwestern fare and décor since it opened in 1992. Mock-cowhide seating, faux adobe walls and buffalo-blazoned light fixtures create the air of a Rio Grande hacienda. Lighter and less expensive fare (enchiladas, quesadillas, and chili—try the steak and black bean or the eight-vegetable version) is served upstairs at the **Border Café**. The downstairs grill features a more elaborate menu, from grilled Colorado lamb chops to roasted red-chili-and-pecan-crusted chicken breast served with plantains and black-bean empanadas.

### TenPenh                                       $$$   Southeast Asian

*1001 Pennsylvania Ave. NW. Closed Sun. 202-393-4500. www.tenpenh.com.*

The sumptuous décor and notable flavors of one of Washington, DC's most popular Asian restaurants resulted from a six-week shopping and tasting journey to South Asia. Begin with the Thai-style coconut and chicken soup with portabella mushrooms before moving on to the macadamia-and-panko-crusted halibut or the red Thai curry prawns. Wash your selection down with sake or ginger limeade.

## Vidalia
$$$ Regional American

*1990 M St. NW. 202-659-1990.*

With upscale versions of shrimp and grits and chicken and dumplings, Vidalia is an oasis of Southern comfort food in Washington's bustling business district. Vidalia's contemporary Southern design complements the warm cornbread and refreshing lemonade that accent a summer lunch. Try the signature roasted Vidalia onion in season, and end your meal with sticky pecan pie topped with bourbon-laced ice cream.

# Budget

## Bangkok Bistro
$$ Thai

*3251 Prospect St. NW. 202-337-2424.*

The smooth lines and soothing violet and green colors of Bangkok Bistro won an award from Architectural Digest. With its outdoor cafe and garden seating, the Georgetown restaurant invites a lively summer dining crowd, while the fiery Thai flavors sizzle all year long. Bangkok Bistro eschews potent chiles for subtler flavors in its best dishes.

## Café Deluxe
$$ American

*3228 Wisconsin Ave. NW. 202-686-2233. www.cafedeluxe.com.*

With the feel of a trendy brasserie, Café Deluxe eases patrons into a menu of traditional comfort foods. Soothing, dark booths provide a relaxing backdrop for the grilled meatloaf with Creole sauce and applewood-smoked pork chops, while the contrasting Art Deco décor complements new renditions of old cocktails, such as Imperial martinis, made with a splash of chambord. Café Deluxe placates vegetarians with generous salads, pastas and pizzas smothered with vegetables and cheese. Gooey apple pie with caramel sauce will please most any sweet tooth.

## Clyde's of Georgetown
$$ American

*3236 M St. NW. 202-333-9180. www.clydes.com.*

With several locations in the Washington metropolitan area, cheery, saloon-like Clyde's has burgeoned into a Washington legend. Casual diners can opt for traditional burgers, sandwiches and chili, while patrons with greater expectations can select from a lengthy list of fashionable martinis and fresh seafood. The bar's a happening singles scene on weekends.

## Lauriol Plaza
$$ Mexican

*1835 18th St. NW. 202-387-0035. www.lauriolplaza.com.*

One of Dupont Circle's most popular eateries, Lauriol Plaza serves up some of the best margaritas in town. Fabulous fajitas and other Tex-Mex mainstays are joined by Puerto Rican and Latin American selections on the extensive menu. With ample outdoor dining, Lauriol Plaza sizzles on summer evenings.

## Lebanese Taverna
$$ Middle Eastern

*2641 Connecticut Ave. NW. 202-265-8681. www.lebanesetaverna.com.*

One of the most popular restaurants in Woodley Park, Lebanese Taverna teems with young professionals and outdoor cafe enthusiasts. Large groups can begin with a savory array of mezze, a spread of hors d'oeuvres, paired with the warm, soft pita bread that emerges from the wood-burning ovens. Try the juicy rotisserie chicken or the lemony chicken *shish taouk*.

## Old Europe
$$ German

*2434 Wisconsin Ave. NW.  202-333-7600.  www.old-europe.com.*

One of Washington's only German restaurants, Old Europe draws a healthy contingency of beer and schnitzel lovers who find solace in few other locales. The walls are covered, as you might expect, with steins and wooden crests that create a perpetual air of Oktoberfest. Satisfying, hearty dishes are served up in short order by the friendly waitstaff.

## Old Glory
$$ Barbecue

*3139 M St. NW. 202-337-3406. www.oldglorybbq.com.*

Don't miss this lively barbecue joint perched on the busy Georgetown corner of M Street and Wisconsin Avenue. Settle into a booth, and a server will promptly arrive to "brand" your table with a purposeful slap of an iron stamp. Each table comes equipped with six regionally-inspired sauces to suit patrons' preferences. Mosey up to the lavish hickory bar, where you'll find the largest selection of bourbons in DC. Kids favor the draft root beer.

## Tortilla Coast
$$ Tex-Mex

*400 First St. SE. Closed Sun. 202-546-6768. www.tortillacoast.com.*

Wayward Texans have found their way to Tortilla Coast for potent margaritas and spicy tastes of home since 1988. Cleanse your palate with the Stars and Stripes margarita, a blend of traditional and strawberry margaritas laced with Blue Curacao. Southwestern flavors shine through in the hickory barbecue chicken fajitas, while spinach and mushroom enchiladas satisfy vegetarians.

## Zaytinya
$$ Mediterranean

*701 9th St. NW (at G St.). 202-638-0800. www.zaytinya.com.*

Both the food and the color scheme at Zaytinya evokes the sun-drenched Mediterranean region. A relative newcomer, the boisterous restaurant has drawn rave reviews since it opened in 2002. Savor small servings ("mezze") of braised rabbit with lentils, cured Turkish loin of beef, and shredded chicken salad with walnut sauce, or splurge on the fresh fish of the day, grilled whole. Desserts meld exotic flavors in the likes of warm semolina cake with yogurt sorbet and cardamom sauce, and Medjool dates roasted in Greek Vinsanto (sweet wine) with orange shortbread and olive-oil ice cream.

## Ben's Chili Bowl
$ Chili

*1213 U St. NW. 202-667-0909. www.benschilibowl.com.*

Ben's is the common meeting ground for DC's traditional African-American community and young urban dwellers. Sloppy chili dogs, thick milkshakes and fries loaded with cheese and chili have proven to be universal pleasers in this Washington dining landmark. The interior retains the nostalgic charm of a 1950s diner, while attracting modern business types for power lunches. Comedian Bill Cosby's favorite is the chili half-smoke.

## Brickskeller
$ American

*1523 22nd St. NW. 202-293-1885. www.thebrickskellar.com.*

Even before microbreweries were the rage, this simple bar with checkered tablecloths was well known to beer aficionados. Its drink menu—really a booklet—is broken down by countries, with all available beers from a particular nation listed. The hundreds of brews available range from Belgium Trappist ale to Lebanese Almaza. Little wonder that owner Dave Alexander holds the Guiness world record for the "most varieties of beer commercially available."

## Firehook Bakery & Coffeehouse
$ Bakery

*3411 Connecticut Ave. NW. 202-362-2253. www.firehook.com. Check Web site for other locations.*

For a quick, tasty sandwich or a sugary snack, Firehook Bakery captures carbohydrate fiends with its tempting window displays. Mini-loaves of fresh, crusty bread compliment fresh mozzarella and pesto on a simple tomato and mozzarella sandwich, while cream-filled tarts beg to be taken home from behind old-fashioned glass cases.

## Oodles Noodles $ Asian

*1120 19th St. NW. 202-293-3138.*

Oodles Noodles lives up to its name by playfully fusing Malaysian, Japanese, Indonesian, Thai and Chinese variations of noodles. Select from udon, ramen, egg, and chow fun noodles, then select a preparation style—the frenzied cooks do the rest. Savory satays and chicken-coconut soup are worthy introductions to a quick, simple menu.

## Pizzeria Paradiso $ Pizza

*2029 P St. NW. 202-223-1245.*

Tucked inside a tiny row house near Dupont Circle, Pizzeria Paradiso's delicate crust and fresh ingredients join forces to create one of the best pizzas in the nation's capital. Its new location in Georgetown is twice as big *(3282 M St. NW; 202-337-1245)*. Exceptional crust soaks in a smoky flavor from the wood-burning oven, as fresh mozzarella melts over a bed of thinly sliced roma tomatoes.

## Rockland's Barbeque and Grilling Company $ Barbecue

*2418 Wisconsin Ave. NW. 202-333-2556. www.rocklands.com.*

For a quick, inexpensive meal in upper Georgetown, follow the sweet smell of hickory smoke up Wisconsin Avenue to Rocklands. Traditional barbecue staples, from ribs and chopped pork to jalapeño cornbread, are deftly handled here. If you're shopping for something a little different, try the smoky grilled catfish or salmon sandwich.

## Saigonnais $ Vietnamese

*2307 18th St. NW. 202-232-5300. www.dcnet.com/saigonnais.*

Located in the heart of Adams Morgan, Saigonnais tantalizes with aromatic Indochine creations. Stylish and simple, the spring rolls are crisp and flavorful, while the pork-filled crêpe rolls (some assembly required) offer a challenging prelude to the suave lemongrass chicken and other generous dishes. The walls of the tiny restaurant are covered with photos of celebrity patrons.

*The properties listed below were selected for their ambience, location and/or value for money. Prices reflect the average cost for a standard double room for two people (not including applicable taxes). You can often find discounted rates on weekends and off-season. Properties are located in Washington, DC, unless otherwise specified. Quoted rates don't include the city's hotel tax of 14.5%. For a complete listing of hotels mentioned in this guide, see Index.*

| | | | |
|---|---|---|---|
| $$$$$ | over $300 | $$ | $75–$125 |
| $$$$ | $200–$300 | $ | less than $75 |
| $$$ | $125–$200 | | |

## Luxury

### Four Seasons Hotel                    $$$$$    257 rooms

*2800 Pennsylvania Ave. NW. 202-342-0444 or 800-332-3442. www.fourseasons.com.*

With an unassuming brick exterior, this upscale hotel earns its distinguished marks with the luxury and impeccable service you'd expect from Four Seasons. Original art adorns the walls of the roomy suites, complimenting the tony flavor of surrounding Georgetown. Take advantage of the state-of-the-art fitness center, or treat yourself to a massage at the spa.

### The Ritz Carlton Washington, DC          $$$$$    300 rooms

*1150 22nd St. NW. 202-835-0500 or 800-241-3333. www.ritzcarlton.com.*

The addition of the Ritz to the Washington luxury hotel landscape brings sought-after amenities to the West End. Large rooms are bathed in mossy tones, with sumptuous bedding and upscale perks—an overnight shoeshine and complimentary morning newspaper—which appeal to business travelers. Guests can work out and have a relaxing massage at the Sports Club/LA Splash sports complex (see Spas).

### The Fairmont Washington, DC $$$$ 415 rooms

*2401 M St. NW. 202-429-2400 800-441-1414. www.fairmont.com.*

The great outdoors reigns in the Fairmont, as sunlight pours through the glassed-in atriums where trees flourish. Ample guest rooms are clothed in elegant furnishings and sunny hues; posh executive suites are tailored to suit business travelers and to accommodate small meetings. Ideally located on the fringes of Georgetown, the Fairmont provides easy access to shops and restaurants.

### Hay-Adams $$$$ 145 rooms

*16th & H Sts. NW. 202-638-6600 or 800-424-5054. www.hayadams.com.*

With a picturesque view of the Executive Mansion from its location across Lafayette Square, the Hay-Adams is closer to the White House than any other of Washington's grand dame hotels. Steeped in Washington lore, this 1928 Renaissance-inspired beauty repeatedly houses world leaders and discerning travelers. Rooms reflect the tailored elegance of a private home; some have carved plaster ceilings and balconies overlooking Lafayette Square.

### Hotel George $$$$ 139 rooms

*15 E St. NW. 202-347-4200 or 800-576-8331. www.hotelgeorge.com.*

Washington's hippest hotel stormed onto the DC scene in 1998 to the chagrin of hotel traditionalists and to the delight of style-hungry liberals. With vibrant colors and contemporary artistic tributes to the first President of the United States, the Hotel George's very vogue minimalist interior and its proximity to Union Station have made it a staple of business and leisure travelers and celebrity guests. The decisively French **Bistro Bis ($$$)** swarms with politicos and Washington celebrities.

## Hotel Washington      $$$$   344 rooms

*515 15th St. NW. 202-638-5900 or 800-424-9540. www.hotelwashington.com.*

Sporting one of the best views of Washington atop its rooftop Sky Terrace, the Hotel Washington sits a mere block and a half from the White House. Luxurious appointments include marble bathrooms, classic window treatments and spectacular views of historic Pennsylvania Avenue. Guests here can enjoy the sauna, fitness center and hair salon.

## Jefferson Hotel      $$$$   100 rooms

*1200 16th St. NW. 202-347-2200 or 800-368-5966. www.thejeffersondc.com.*

Dignitaries and diplomats favor this Beaux-Arts landmark. Built as a grand private residence in 1923, the Jefferson dazzles with its established reputation and classic exterior. A cheery courtyard leads into a Federal-style lobby. Individually decorated guest rooms boast period antiques; some even have four-poster beds and fireplaces. Keep an eye out for original documents signed by Thomas Jefferson himself, which are displayed throughout the hotel.

## The Latham Hotel      $$$$   143 rooms

*3000 M St. NW. 202-726-5000 or 800-368-5922. www.thelatham.com.*

With a primo Georgetown location that houses Citronelle (see Must Eat), one of Washington's most revered restaurants, the Latham's comfy guest rooms and rambling suites readily impress. The hotel boasts nine unique, two-story carriage suites and elegantly appointed guest rooms complete with terrycloth robes, marble baths, large desks and shaving mirrors.

## The Madison Hotel      $$$$   341 rooms

*15th & M Sts. NW. 202-862-1600 or 800-424-8577. www.themadisonhotel.net.*

Perhaps better known for its graceful collection of antiques, the Madison proudly markets itself as "Washington's Correct Address." Located just a few blocks from the White House, the Madison's guest rooms are beautifully decorated with custom-made Federal-style furnishings. The hotel reopened in August 2003 following a $30 million renovation.

## Renaissance Mayflower Hotel      $$$$   660 rooms

*1127 Connecticut Ave. NW. 202-347-3000 or 800-468-3571. www.renaissancehotels.com.*

Opened in 1925, the venerable Mayflower is a perennial favorite of frequent visitors. The hotel flaunts the splendor of Washington's golden age along busy Connecticut Avenue, near museums, the White House, shopping and restaurants. The lobby of Washington's largest luxury hotel is graced with Beaux-Arts furniture and gilded accents, while the guest rooms recall the gentility of a distant era with their marble bathrooms and antiques.

### St. Regis Washington, DC                    $$$$    193 rooms

*16th & K Sts. NW. 202-638-2626 or 888-627-8087. www.starwood.com/stregis.*

The St. Regis looms over Washington's thriving business district with an air of distinction and aloofness. Inside, it's a glorious window into Washington's history of politics and intrigue. Since Calvin Coolidge cut the ribbon for the hotel's grand opening, every president has stopped by this hotel, which frequently hosts royal guests and rock stars (think Queen Elizabeth II and Mick Jagger).

### The Watergate Hotel    $$$$    250 rooms

*2650 Virginia Ave. NW. 202-965-2300 or 888-737-9477. www.thewatergatehotel.com.*

Few Washington hotels are as cloaked in scandal as the Watergate, but dignity and grace have been restored to the riverside property. The swirling complex on the Potomac River offers stunning river views and easy access to the Kennedy Center and Georgetown. Newly renovated rooms are tastefully decorated, and the rooftop bar serves an enticing summer martini. For exercise, take a few laps in the Olympic-size indoor pool.

### Willard Inter-Continental                   $$$$    341 rooms

*1401 Pennsylvania Ave. NW. 202-628-9100 or 800-827-1747. www.washington.interconti.com.*

A bastion of Washington tradition, the Willard towers over historic Pennsylvania Avenue two blocks from the White House. Inside, the dreamy Beaux-Arts lobby fosters political mystique with its grand columns and glittering chandeliers. The Round Robin Bar has served many a president mint juleps and potent brandies. Recently renovated, rooms reflect a tasteful, antique-drenched opulence, complete with views of the Washington skyline.

## Moderate

### Channel Inn Hotel                            $$$    100 rooms

*650 Water St. SW. 202-554-2400 or 800-368-5668. www.channelinn.com.*

Billed as Washington, DC's only waterfront hotel, the Channel Inn offers comfortable, affordable rooms with breathtaking views of the Washington Marina. Several neighboring seafood restaurants and DC's nearby fresh-fish market accentuate the riverside hotel with fresh catches and homemade flavors. Airy rooms offer full amenities and inviting balconies on which to watch graceful sailboats and river cruise ships glide past.

### Embassy Square

$$$   278 rooms

*2000 N St. NW. 202-659-9000 or 800-424-2999. www.embassysquare.com.*

Surrounded by colorful Dupont Circle's unpredictable sights and sounds, the Embassy Square is a simple, comfortable retreat ideally located near attractions, shops, restaurants and nightlife. The spacious suites are adorned with dark woods and deep green tones. You'll enjoy a complimentary continental breakfast each morning.

### Georgetown Inn

$$$   96 rooms

*131 Wisconsin Ave. NW. 202-333-8900 or 800-368-5922. www.georgetowninn.com.*

Combining European elegance and colonial charm, the Georgetown Inn sits along bustling Wisconsin Avenue, in the heart of tony Georgetown's shops and restaurants. Luxurious marble bathrooms and heavenly four-poster beds lend an air of regal warmth to a hotel that has housed the Duke and Duchess of Windsor during past visits to Washington, DC.

### Georgetown Suites

$$$   217 rooms

*1111 30th St. NW. 202-298-7800 or 800-348-7203. www.georgetownsuites.com.*

Perfect for families and long-term visitors, this all-suite hotel is just minutes from historic Georgetown's shops and restaurants. Spacious comfortable suites come with fully equipped kitchenettes generously outfitted with microwaves, dishwashers and icemakers. Contemporary furnishings and pastel tones characterize the soothing décor.

### Henley Park Hotel

$$$   96 rooms

*926 Massachusetts Ave. NW. 202-638-5200 or 800-222-8474. www.henleypark.com.*

The Henley Park Hotel's Tudor-style exterior and meticulously restored rooms reflect the classic elegance of Washington's earlier days. Less than a block from the Washington Convention Center, the Henley Park offers complimentary limo service to downtown or Capitol Hill. Gargoyles guard the entrance to this charming hotel, which prides itself on its attentive service.

### Hotel Lombardy

$$$   132 rooms

*2019 Pennsylvania Ave. NW. 202-828-2600 or 800-424-5486. www.hotellombardy.com.*

Restored to reflect its original 1929 character, the Hotel Lombardy is located just four blocks from the White House in the center of Washington's business district. Sumptuous bedding compliments the densely woven oriental rugs and sleek chrome bath fixtures. Technological amenities coexist with the quaint ambience of this bastion of traditional DC hospitality.

### Hotel Monticello of Georgetown

$$$   47 suites

*1075 Thomas Jefferson St. NW. 202-337-0900 or 800-388-2410. www.hotelmonticello.com.*

The Hotel Monticello's sunny suites brim with European charm and Georgetown sophistication. Just footsteps from the starting point of the historic C&O Canal and lively Wisconsin Avenue, the Monticello's ample rooms provide an excellent base for exploring Georgetown. You'll find Hermes products in the marble baths, and room rates include a continental breakfast.

### Hotel Rouge $$$ 137 rooms

*1315 16th St. NW. 202-232-8000 or 800-738-1202. www.rougehotel.com.*

You can't help but see red at this luxury boutique property on Embassy Row. True to its name, red is the color theme carried throughout the edgy décor of the lobby, the rooms and the sleek Bar Rouge. You'll even be welcomed with a complimentary Bloody Mary when you check in. If you feel like cooking, the hotel offers Chow Rooms, equipped with stainless-steel kitchenettes. Just want to kick back? Chill Rooms feature two 27-inch Sony flat-screen TVs and a Sony PlayStation that doubles as a DVD player.

### Jurys Washington $$$ 314 rooms

*1500 New Hampshire Ave. NW. 202-483-6000 or 800-423-6953. www.jurysdoyle.com.*

Flanking Washington's beloved Dupont Circle, the Jurys Washington's spacious guest rooms boast technological amenities geared to business travelers, including a business center, voice mail and a trouser press. Along the circle, Dupont Grille and Biddy Mulligan's bar reflect the hotel's Irish ownership, complimenting the cosmopolitan neighborhood spirit.

### The Melrose Hotel $$$ 240 rooms

*2430 Pennsylvania Ave. NW. 202-955-6400 or 800-635-7673. www.melrosehotel.com.*

Sporting a catchy new name and fresh look, the Melrose reopened its doors in Foggy Bottom after an extensive remodeling project. The rooms bespeak comfortable luxury, while nightly rates have not raced to catch up. Located near George Washington University within walking distance of the Kennedy Center and Georgetown, the Melrose's sunny, cheery rooms are a Washington bargain.

### Monaco Hotel
$$$   184 rooms

*700 F St. NW. 202-628-7177 or 800-649-1202. www.monaco-dc.com.*

Located in the revitalized Penn Quarter downtown, the Monaco occupies the restored 1893 Neoclassical Tariff Building. In the guest rooms, you'll find 15ft ceilings and sunny yellow walls accented by bright contemporary furnishings. The National Portrait Gallery is right across the street, as is the sports and entertainment megaplex, MCI Center. Pets are welcome here, but if Fido couldn't make the trip, you can have a goldfish delivered to your room to keep you company. Oh-so-chic Poste ($$$) American brasserie next door provides 24-hour room service.

### Morrison-Clark Inn
$$$   54 rooms

*1015 L St. NW. 202-898-1200 or 800-332-7898. www.morrisonclark.com.*

This turn-of-the-century mansion seems misplaced in the middle of downtown's business district. Past the antiques-filled parlor, with lace curtains and burgundy wall coverings, you'll find three styles of accommodations. Choose from neutral-toned Neoclassical, opulent Victorian, and country-style distressed woods and wicker. The restaurant's ($$$) seasonal American cuisine has made it a local favorite.

### Washington Court Hotel
$$$   264 rooms

*525 New Jersey Ave. NW. 202-628-2100 or 800-321-3010. www.washingtoncourthotel.com*

Luxurious suites offer an unparalleled view of the Capitol dome in this charming Capitol Hill hotel. Independently operated, the Washington Court Hotel provides easy access to Washington's monuments, attractions and restaurants. There's a full business center in the lobby and a state-of-the-art fitness room on the third floor.

## Budget

### Doolittle Guest House
$$   3 rooms

*506 E. Capitol St. NE. 202-546-6622. www.doolittlehouse.com.*

Though situated on a quiet, tree-lined street, this 1866 Victorian stands only four blocks from the US Capitol. From here, guests can walk to almost all DC attractions, including the Smithsonian museums on the Mall and the Union Station train terminal. Three antique-appointed guest rooms and a library stocked with magazines and newspapers make for a comfortable night's stay. Breakfasts prepared with local produce and a gourmet's flair provide fuel for a day of sightseeing.

## Hotel Tabard Inn

$$ 40 rooms

*1739 N St. NW. 202-785-1277. www.tabardinn.com*

A Dupont Circle institution for 80 years, this
hotel oozes charm with its scarlet walls, twisting
staircases, stained-glass lamps and heavy antique
furnishings. You have to walk up to your room
here (there's no elevator). Eclectic guest quarters
vary in size and décor; some share bathrooms. For
lunch or dinner, you can savor acclaimed New

American fare at the inn's acclaimed **restaurant ($$$)** in the simple dining room
or in the walled garden. A continental breakfast is included in the room tab.

## Allen Lee Hotel

$ 85 rooms

*2224 F St. NW. 202-331-1224 or 800-462-0186. www.allenleehotel.com.*

If you don't mind going without the frills of a big hotel, the Allen Lee is a great
value. Its location near George Washington University in Foggy Bottom lies
within easy walking distance of Georgetown shopping and nightlife, as well as
the White House and the museums on the Mall (or you can always catch the
Metrorail just four blocks away.) All rooms have phones and TVs; the least
expensive rooms share a bath.

## Braxton Hotel

$ 62 rooms

*1440 Rhode Island Ave. NW, between 14th & 15th Sts. 202-232-7800 or 800-350-5759.
www.braxtonhotel.com.*

You can't beat the location for the price at this small hotel, located just six
blocks from the White House on a quiet, tree-lined street. Well-appointed
rooms all come with refrigerators and TV with HBO (movies available for an
extra fee). If you need a microwave, a hair dryer or an iron and ironing board,
just ask.

## Hereford House

$ 4 rooms

*604 South Carolina Ave. SE. 202-543-0102. www.bbonline.com/dc/hereford.*

English hospitality welcomes guests at this Capitol Hill B&B. Settle back in the
parlor, have a proper cup of tea, and let owner Ann Edwards fill you in on what
to see and do in the neighborhood—the Capitol and the Library of Congress
are just a pleasant 10-minute walk away. Four individually decorated rooms—
with no TVs or phones to bother you—share two baths. You'll start your day
off right here with a hearty complimentary breakfast. Pets are allowed with
permission, but this property doesn't cotton to kids under 12.

## Kalorama Guest House

$ 30 rooms

*1854 Mintwood Pl. NW. 202-667-6369. www.washingtonpost.com/yp/kgh.*

Nestled in culturally diverse Adams Morgan, this charming assortment of
Victorian townhouses pampers visitors with homey comforts, such as afternoon sherry and tasty continental breakfast selections. Rooms are sparse and
simple, tinged with Victorian flair that mirrors the vibrant and well-loved
neighborhood.

# Index

The following abbreviations may appear in this Index: NHS National Historic Site; NM National Monument; NMem National Memorial; NP National Park; NHP National Historical Park; NWR National Wildlife Refuge; SP State Park; SHP State Historic Park; SHS State Historic Site.

# Index

# Index

## Photos Courtesy Of: